A STATE OF FEAR

A
STATE OF
FEAR

ANDREW
GRAHAM-YOOLL

Memories of Argentina's Nightmare

ELAND, LONDON
&
HIPPOCRENE BOOKS, INC., NEW YORK

Published by
ELAND
53 Eland Road, London SW11 5JX
&
HIPPOCRENE BOOKS, INC.,
171 Madison Avenue, New York, NY 10016

First issued in this edition 1986
© Andrew Graham-Yooll 1986

British Library Cataloguing in Publication Data

Graham-Yooll, Andrew
A state of fear: memories of Argentina's
nightmare.
1. Argentina—Politics and government—
1955–1983   2. Argentina—Politics and
government—1983–
I. Title
982'.064'0924   F2849.2

ISBN 0–907871–51–8
ISBN 0–907871–36–4 Pbk

Photoset, printed and bound in Great Britain by
Redwood Burn Limited,
Trowbridge, Wiltshire

Cover illustration © Tony Ansell
Cover design © Patrick Frean

To Micaela
who lived this book with me

BIOGRAPHY

Andrew Graham-Yooll was born in 1944 in Argentina and went to school in Buenos Aires and Montevideo. He started in journalism on the *Buenos Aires Herald* in 1966 and spent the next ten years there, eventually to become one of the best known political writers in Argentina, a position which was eventually to force him to leave the country in 1976 – after a particularly brutal military dictatorship seized power. It is that period which takes up most of *A State of Fear*. In London in 1976, he first joined the *Daily Telegraph* for a short time, and from there moved to *The Guardian* where he spent nearly seven years. In 1984 he became deputy editor of *South* (The Third World Magazine) and editor in 1985.

Andrew Graham-Yooll has published over a dozen books, in Argentina, Venezuela, Spain and the United States, as well as in the United Kingdom. His books in English include *The Press in Argentina 1973–1978* (1979); *The Forgotten Colony: a history of the English-speaking communities in Argentina* (1981), *Portrait of an Exile* (1981), and *Small wars you may have missed* (1983). Each has become a standard work of reference on its subject.

ACKNOWLEDGEMENTS

A State of Fear was first published in part as *Portrait of an Exile* by Junction Books, London, in 1981. Various passages have previously been published in the *Partisan Review, London Magazine, International Herald Tribune, Literary Review, New Scientist,* and *Index on Censorship.*

Note: Some identities, place names, and references to specific events have been altered to protect individuals, or to avoid causing them embarrassment.

CHRONOLOGY

1930 – September: Army general, José Felix Uriburu, leads a coup
d'état against the constitutionally elected President
Hipólito Yrigoyen (of the Civic Radical Union) and installs
a military government for two years.

1943 – June: A military coup overthrows the conservative civilian
government and paves the way for Colonel Juan Perón to
take office three years later.

1945 – March: Argentina enters World War II and declares war on
Germany, after remaining neutral throughout the
hostilities.

1946 – February: General Juan Perón enters government as
constitutionally-elected president.

1947 – February: Argentina nationalises the British owned
railways.

1952 – July: Evita, Eva María Duarte de Perón, wife of the
President, dies of leukaemia.

1955 – September: President Perón is overthrown by a military
coup.

1958 – February: constitutional administration is restored and
Arturo Frondizi is elected president.

1962 – March: Arturo Frondizi is overthrown by a military coup.
A military-backed civilian administration remains as
caretaker until elections in 1963.

1966 – June: the constitutional administration of President Arturo
Illia is overthrown by a military coup.

1973 – May: President Héctor Cámpora takes over as
constitutionally-elected President at the end of the military
regime.

1973 – July: President Cámpora is removed by his own Peronist
Party. A caretaker government holds new elections in
September.

1973 – October: General Juan Perón takes office as constitutionally-elected president.
1974 – July: President Juan Perón dies. His widow, María Estela Martinez Cartas de Perón ('Isabelita'), succeeds him.
1976 – March: a military coup d'état removes Mrs Perón from government.
1982 – April–June: Argentina invades the Falkland Islands and is defeated by Britain.
1983 – December: President Raúl Alfonsín enters office as constitutionally-elected chief executive at the end of the military dictatorship.

CONTENTS

Chapter

1

A PRESS CONFERENCE

June 1973

After the initial greeting, after the pleasure of seeing him again
– a man for whose release from prison I had campaigned as far
as self-censorship and my own limited guts permitted – he sat
on the chair by my desk. He put his elbows on his knees and
looked down, took a long pull on his cigarette and blew a jet
of smoke at the floor.

'How would you like to be kidnapped?' he asked, without
looking up. Ten or fifteen heartbeats jolted my body. They
filled my ears to deafness, reddened my face. The sound
mixed with the thought of how worried my wife would be;
whether the paper could afford a ransom; what the editor
would say about my suddenly disappearing and whether I
could go with so much of the paper still to be done. When the
noise in my ears subsided I asked feeby, 'Now?'

'No, for Christ's sake... Let's arrange a time and a place.'

The time of this story is in the distant dullness of undesirable
memories which can become unnervingly vivid, then subside.
The events are filed away with my dismay at the refinement of
cruelty; with my anger at the stupidity of immolation of
young men and women, of old school chums and newsroom
mates, of the parents of my children's friends... They are
filled with my bewilderment at the brutality of guerrilla action
and counter-action in the place where I was born, Argentina.
Life was easy, though often parochial, even in the largest
cities, where the narrowness of views and absence of rational
thought reflect the shallowness of oft-claimed cosmopolita-
nism. I am still shocked by the folly of youthful rebels. They

found explanations for murder in a tone of voice which sounded like normal discussion in conversation, the outrage hardly noticeable in day-to-day dying, in a country where death is part of life. I am just as overwhelmed by the fury of the backlash; the blind cruelty of the most primitive beings, with the cold calculation of the very cunning.

Cruelty has run through the continent. A continent which European writers have failed to explain and few Latin Americans have succeeded in interpreting.

Now I am thinking of events between 1972 and 1976; but I am beginning to believe that it might have been any five years in the last four centuries. It is not that historical cycles have been repeated; it is just that there have been no cycles; the behaviour has never changed. There was change in the intensity of the action, not in the perspective.

Events put me now so far away from home; home on the south side of Buenos Aires, on the British-run railway line in a village built as a watering stop for British-built steam engines; where the evening train stopped at twenty-past-six, pre-established by an English manager of the Southern Railway traffic office, who thought half-past-six was the right time for the day's first gin and tonic. It seems a whole era away from the annual outings of our village English School to the English pantomime in the city. This outing by the Ranelagh Community School (Ranelagh being fourteen miles south of Buenos Aires, not in south-west London) took place each year on Empire Day, the very eve of Argentina's Liberty Day. Afterwards, we wrote essays – about Empire Day, of course.

He looked up, noticed my discomfort, and said: 'We want to talk to you. We want you to come.'

He sat by my desk, the news editor's desk, in the *Buenos Aires Herald*, Argentina's centenarian English-language daily newspaper, next door to the English Club. He stood and walked across the newsroom to a large wall-plan of the city of Buenos Aires. His finger pointed to a little green box, a park, a few blocks from the Plaza Constitución terminal of what used to be called the Southern Railway (*Ferro Carril Sud*) and is now the General Roca Line of the Argentine National Railways.

'I'll meet you there. At ten o'clock in the morning,' he told me. It was an order. I made a protest about the time, because I usually went to bed at 3 a.m. But I knew that my curiosity, his orders – he was a few years younger than I: a pip-squeak giving me orders – and my pride would combine to get me there on time.

He had surprised me with his visit. He had been out of prison only a few days, freed under the amnesty decreed in his first hours in office by our new President, Héctor Cámpora.

My visitor had walked into the newsroom with the air of a person who knew it. As he walked towards my desk by the window I had risen with my arms opening and a smile on my face. 'Keep your voice down,' he had snapped, with a thin smile. I had dropped into my chair.

I told him I was delighted to see him, remarked that he looked too thin. He had always been thin; but he had become anaemic in prison. He had been arrested one year before, accused of driving the car used in the kidnapping of the managing director of a car manufacturing subsidiary in Argentina.

My friend's arrest in a flat in San Telmo, the old South side of the city, as evidence of his political activism, had come as a surprise to many of us. I remembered him from parties in the late sixties, usually parties which gathered fashionable writers, playwrights, artists and publishers. My wife and I were not fashionable, but somehow were invited anyway. He had been there, collecting praise as one of the better magazine journalists, writing on events concerning the Tupamaro guerrillas in Uruguay and the international arms market. His girlfriend in those days was a beautiful young woman who would go to those parties in the very short shorts, 'hot pants', then fashionable. I remembered sitting by her on the floor, in conversation, my eyes straying down the length of her long, white legs. The couple had parted that year – it must have been about 1970 – as politics entered their lives and took them separate ways. He went into the vernacular Marxist People's Rev-

15

olutionary Army; she into trade union activism (and later into the press and propaganda section of the nationalist Auténtico Party, the surface branch of the Montoneros guerrillas. In 1976, police would go to a meeting of party officers and she would be killed with several others).

Two days later, on a rainy wintry morning in June 1973, I set out for the prearranged abduction. Before leaving our home in Acassuso, half an hour north of the city, I told my wife not only where I was going, but also where the insurance policy was; which publishers had what of mine and at what stage of printing; whom to call, in case of 'problems'; and other precautions one takes at times such as the eve of departure on a business trip or an aeroplane flight on holiday. But we hoped nothing would happen.

How could anything happen? These were people whom we used to meet at parties; the idea of guns in their hands was too remote, too theoretical. It is true that some of them killed, some of them got killed, but I had not yet seen a body ripped to bits by bullets, and so it all seemed a little inconceivable. The idea that I could stand around talking to people who killed and then discussed death as part of politics had not yet entered my field of political writing. It was 1973, and, politically, I was half-baked. Friends had been arrested, friends of friends had been killed. Even I had been arrested as a reporter once. A drunken policeman had once fired a shot rather close to me in Ranelagh, years ago; and even my father, in anger at my careless handling of a pistol, had fired a shot from a .22 Smith & Wesson between my legs, when I was ten. But it was all part of living, not of dying.

It was still drizzling as I came out of the underground in Plaza Constitución, a grey building that is not too distantly related to Victoria Station, but facing a lifeless park with a tile pavement around the perimeter, and tile pavements crossing diagonally and meeting at a bare tile area in the centre.

It was only a few blocks to the rendezvous, another desolate square with tile pavements around the perimeter and tile pavements crossing diagonally... This part of town, loved as a warm 'barrio' by its residents, looked hostile to the outsider with its smelly food stores, which had spotty mirrors, cold stone counter-tops and floors covered with sawdust to take up the damp from the patrons' wet shoes. The rows of assignation hotels along Santiago del Estero street fell behind and made way to the fortress-like flat-roof houses with deep doorways (often leading into beautiful patios) and tall shuttered windows which were opened only for a girl's fifteenth birthday party, or a wedding; and then were shut again for years.

Close to the square he came into sight, walking towards me, looking even thinner than when he had come to the newsroom, as the rain plastered his hair down on his forehead, and his shoulders, hunched forward, drooped away from the upturned collar of his coat. As I looked at him, skipping over puddles, I wondered why anybody might ever think he could be a killer.

There was a strange feeling in my stomach. Some people call what I assume is a similar feeling to them, a knot. Others call it butterflies. It is a kind of sudden emptiness, in spite of any recent meal, and I had had a normal breakfast an hour before.

'It is raining,' he informed me as we crossed. 'You better go for a cup of coffee.' He said there was a bar just around the corner and I would be fetched there. I asked if anything had gone wrong.

'I'm going to get some petrol for the car.' I guffawed with relief at the normality of such a difficulty. Later I was annoyed that even on such a minor issue as transport there was need to distort the truth. I had been summoned early so that I could be watched, and so that transportation arrangements could be made in safety.

In the tiny corner café, sitting at a table, were a reporter from an Argentine morning paper, a staff reporter from the Buenos Aires office of a United States news agency, and a roving correspondent of the Madrid newspaper *Pueblo*. Two patrons were at the bar counter, talking to the proprietor. We

17

kept the Espresso machine hissing for the next forty-five minutes with several rounds of coffee. Two of us ordered large 'especiales' sandwiches, ham and cheese in a French roll. I was not the only one with a feeling of emptiness.

Before President Cámpora's inauguration and the amnesty for political prisoners, guerrilla press conferences had seldom been held; interviews with guerrilla chiefs had been almost impossible to arrange, except for foreign correspondents who came and went. When guerrillas had wanted to say something – usually to mark a special occasion, because ordinary statements on action were made by telephone or by post – they had carried off one or two journalists, blindfolded. The 'conference' had usually been held in a moving van or car to avoid using any location. The name of kidnapping remained; but like so much jargon adjusted to political requirements, it was believed by nobody. So many words have a double meaning in Argentine politics...

After about half-an-hour we were joined by a young man. He had short neatly-combed hair and chubby cheeks; he wore a smart raincoat, underneath which was an open-neck shirt. This dark-faced gentleman had obviously never been to prison and, in fact, had probably kept a regular job without any need to lose the cover. Our new companion ordered a cup of coffee and a sandwich and offered us something to drink, which we refused. After another fifteen minutes he stood, paid his bill and told us to get ready, coinciding exactly with the arrival of a small, very old school bus, painted in regulation bright orange. We were told to get into the bus quickly and the chubby chap left the café last. As we were climbing the three steps into the bus, the running engine back-fired and we thought of a shot. But the thought was gone before it took shape. The middle-aged driver, and two young men with him, took us, jolting and shaking, for about fifteen blocks. Conversation, had we been less tense and desired it, was made impossible anyway by the rattling noise of the bus.

The bus parked outside a large depot-like building, with huge metal doors. As we got out, another man came onto the bus and paid the driver, who was obviously not aware of who we were or what was going on.

We went through a small side door into a large, square, sombre room. It was a dance hall, one of dozens in the district, run by Spaniards catering to their community. We were told that the old couple at the bar at the far side of the room had been informed that the premises, rented by our hosts, were to be used for the purpose of holding a press conference to launch a literary magazine.

Our hosts, four in all – although we later learned that there were three more in the street, patrolling the block – invited us to sit down at a cluster of five tables, around which had been set some chairs.

One by one we were sent into the gents' loo, where we were frisked by a man who seemed an expert at going over every inch of the body with flat hands, checking every pocket and every corner of cloth. His hand froze over my right-hand coat pocket. It was a Ventolin anti-asthma aspirator. He asked sternly what it was, the shape unrecognisable. When told, his face relaxed into a one-quarter smile; he muttered a few words of sympathy and remarked on the nuisance of the illness. I felt that he even admired me a little, subconsciously, for he mentioned that it was the ailment Ernesto 'Che' Guevara suffered all his life.

After this introduction, we waited at the table. We were served another round of coffee and glasses of *ginebra*, Dutch gin, and advised that we could use photographic cameras and tape recorders if we wished to. Who was coming? Well, as far as they knew, the chief of the political bureau of the Workers' Revolutionary Party (PRT), the body organising the People's Revolutionary Army (ERP). Who was that? asked the Spaniard in his ignorance. Why, Mario Roberto Santucho, of course.

On that cue, the side door by the large metal door opened and into the tiled-floor dance hall came Santucho, aged 36, previously a certified accountant; followed by his lieutenants, Benito Jorge Urteaga, aged 27, a former office clerk; Enrique Haroldo Gorriarán Merlo, aged 31, formerly an engineer and a one-time member of the Uruguayan Tupamaros organisation, now a commander of the ERP; and Jorge Molina, aged 30, an architect.

Santucho, nicknamed *Robi*, was a figure approaching legend. His appearance hardly lived up to the reputation, but then, it is difficult to say what I expected of his presence. He had dark curly hair, trimmed short; he was slight in build and soft-spoken. All four were clean-shaven, wore casual, well-fitting new clothes. Gorriarán Merlo was balding and had the looks of a middle-class commuter from suburbia; Urteaga had the warm, impish smile of the boy-about-town; Molina, looking a little gaunt, had the air of a Saturday-afternoon rugby-match spectator with his brown jacket and a silk scarf at his neck.

Santucho, a Marxist, had organised the ERP as an irregular army. He had broken out of prison twice in the last three years; once from the Tucumán jail and once, in August 1972, from the top security prison in Rawson, Chubut, from where he, Gorriarán Merlo and four others, had escaped in a hijacked plane to Chile, where they were given safe-conducts to go to Cuba. Allende was then Chile's president.

I remembered how another nineteen who had escaped with them had not reached the airport in time. Among them was Santucho's wife, Ana Villareal, and Gorriarán Merlo's girlfriend, who had both been killed a few days later. In Santiago de Chile, Santucho and Gorriarán Merlo had broken down and cried.

As they came into the dance hall on that wintry June day, again the thought rose in me, not in my mind, but in the stomach, that these men had all killed other men. And yet they seemed charming. They shook hands with their own men, and then all four walked to each of us, politely introducing themselves and briefly asking how we were and if we had found getting there difficult. Their forces had behind them the fame of Robin Hoods who had hijacked dairy trucks for distribution of the goods in shanty towns, had held up lumber yards and building companies to take the materials to working-class areas where families lived in packing-case homes. They were admired by just as many as hated them.

They were charming young gentlemen ... an accountant,

an architect... They are honourable professions ... but I am condoning crime by remembering charm.

The press conference itself was an anti-climax. I was soon to learn that all guerrilla press conferences, like any other, for that matter, were anti-climaxes. They were held to expose a face, to make contact; but very little that was new was ever said. Guerrilla press conferences are special in the preparations, the apprehension, the fear and the uncertainty. And afterwards, there is the knowledge that one is marked. Police call to check one's address, and telephone callers threaten some form of reprisal. Only sympathisers are called to guerrilla press conferences, they say.

We asked questions and received political answers; we even chatted around the cluster of tables. Santucho said he was bitter at his wife's death; but he was not in search of vengeance. He said a political action had ended their love and marriage, so it would have to be political action that gave a meaning to her death and not render it useless. He spoke softly, without ever raising his voice. He showed no irritation at any question, even when we pressed him for details of his organisation's numerical strength. His answer was simply, and repeatedly, that internal security prevented him from replying. His organisation forecast that Dr Cámpora's government would not last (it collapsed after 49 days). He said the ERP held no kidnap victims (which he referred to as detainees) in the cells of 'peoples' prisons' – which we did not believe; but anyway, the thought does arise that it is a ridiculous name for a cage – and he assured us that ERP forces had greased their guns after the amnesty to await political developments.

I did wonder which of my interlocutors might have squeezed a trigger and seen the man in front of him go down, a large red stain spreading and spurting like a leak in a garden hose. What did that man in dialogue with me think and what had he felt? Or was it all so quick that there was hardly time to notice the shock in the other's face, the shock of knowing that death was immediate? There must have been hardly time to be aware that he would be no more, that whatever was said from then on, whatever was done, the man was no more than the body of a dog, run over by a car and flung to the roadside, as seen so often by every road in Argentina.

Somebody would explain that the first time was the worst. A gunbattle was the best time for initiation; a man or woman shooting for the first time at human targets would never know if anyone had been hit, who fired the shot, and how bad the wound. Sometimes, in this kind of fighting, there was no way of knowing. It was different at close range. Friends had to help then, with comfort and constant reminding of the cause. But the fact was that somebody fired a shot and somebody dropped dead and there is no way to explain such evil later.

When these thoughts came, I shut my eyes tightly and wiped my mind clean, like a drunk trying to focus; because, after all, how can one chat almost amicably with people who go around squeezing triggers and knowing the result is death.

The editor would refer to 'my friends' with a sneer, with disgust, with repulsion at the idea of men and women who seemed charming, friendly and with an average sense of humour, and who could kill. They were in the other team, the one playing against the team that society dresses in uniform and licences to kill. And some of them, too, from soldier to general, are often charming, friendly, and have a sense of humour.

It was chatty and friendly. Santucho did not know his legal status, after the amnesty. We, on the other hand, enjoyed talking with one of Argentina's most wanted men. We used the formal *usted* mixed with the colloquial and more intimate *vos* and the whole event was recorded on a small tape recorder. We drank many cups of coffee and small glasses of *ginebra*. There was no display of guns; and the tension of two hours ago had disappeared.

Before parting, we asked if we could have photographs with them, to which they readily agreed. The one reporter who had a camera with him took several pictures. The man from *Pueblo* and I sat with our hosts for a picture because we wanted evidence of the meeting's existence. Santucho, a few months before, had denied the existence of an interview with the correspondent of the Italian newspaper *Corriere della Sera*, who had alleged that the speakers were hooded but that he had recognised the voices.

The parting was as casual but earnest as the arrival. The chiefs left first, then the lower ranked men, until we were left with only one, who told us when we could walk out into the street. The four of us, alone again, shared a taxi back to the centre of town.

The picture and my story were in the *Buenos Aires Herald* next day. It raised me to the rank of super-reporter in many eyes. In many more I seemed to be, and probably still remain, a guerrilla.

Anonymous telephone calls to our home and to the paper, with threats, started later that day.

2
PICTURE FILE
September 1973

The story of how Polo shat himself in the front seat of a car, while a hand squeezed his neck, and the muzzle of a .38 stabbed at the bony part behind his ear, was told at the news agency some time after it happened. Afternoons at the news agency, before those who had been on a day shift went home and those on nights started work, were a time for reunion and gossip. That evening, conversation moved to stories such as Polo's.

A journalist called Marta had recently been abducted and interrogated about an article she had written on secret societies of which the Social Welfare Minister was a member. She had been softened with mock executions at roadsides around Buenos Aires before she was freed, unharmed but shaken. The following month the *Buenos Aires Herald* was raided by police who came for me on suspicion of participation in a guerrilla organisation. I was not there when they came, but arrived later, when the pressure was off. The officer in command of the raid said I looked like a good guy. 'Lucky you were not here when we came. I had orders to give you a ticket.' A 'ticket' was a one-way passage to the mortuary. I said thank you for staying to tell me. They wrecked the cuttings and picture files that I had kept during ten years. Then they took me.

In each case reaction was different. Marta, defiant, called a press conference and left no doubt that her captors were acting under orders from the government. Then she went into hiding. After I was released I kept the same address, the same routine, and crawled back into the newsroom to try to put together what was left of the damaged files. Polo's story was told for the first time during that chat in the agency newsroom.

Polo was a photographer. A newspicture was the source of his troubles. He had taken the photograph, a group picture in the last months of 1972 or early 1973, when the many splinters within the Peronist movement were putting on an appearance of unity for the election campaign. They had their pictures taken in the style of bandits: during the wedding, before the massacre.

In Argentina, the splinters within Peronism—the left-wing Montoneros guerrillas, the conservative 'old guard' politicians aged sixty and over, and the right-wing shock groups that sometimes liaised with the Montoneros in holdups and kidnappings—united for the textbook causes of returning Peronism to government, returning General Juan Perón to Argentina from his comfortable exile in Madrid, and of promoting the canonisation of Evita Perón. The elections took place in March 1973 and the Peronists won by a comfortable margin. An interim Peronist President was installed in May. One month later, in June 1973, Juan Perón returned to Buenos Aires to a gunbattle at Ezeiza airport fought in his name – some say stage-managed in his name – by factions among his followers. Many were shot dead, some were run through with sharp pointed stakes, some were hung by the neck from trees and many were tortured with cigarette ends and beatings. Factions were preparing to grab whatever scraps of power Perón left them.

Polo's group picture of right-wing leaders and Montoneros chiefs was stolen from the files at the news magazine that he worked for. The photograph was cut, so that only the faces of the right-wing gang leaders were left smiling at the camera, and this doctored version was published in a Montoneros' weekly, *El Descamisado* (The Shirtless One) under a banner headline *These are the murderers* in the Ezeiza airport battle. The photographer did not notice it, even though his mutilated photograph under the sensational headline looked out for a week from under every newspaper kiosk in Buenos Aires.

Polo kissed his wife goodbye at mid-morning after the children had gone to school, and asked if she needed anything from the city centre. She answered 'That you be careful', as she always did; then he left their small fourth-floor flat to take a bus to the news magazine. His building was a marble-slabbed, flat-fronted edifice, with large double-leaf front doors, two lifts and eighty apartments; the same, give or take a few details, as so many other buildings in Buenos Aires, which had shot up like so many unnaturally-tall tree stumps between the squat single-storey buildings which remained from an earlier age.

He thought his stomach felt a little delicate, something he had eaten perhaps; but the unsettled feeling was offset by the warm spring morning in that September of 1973. He started thinking of the day's work. It would probably be something political again. Political activity, between formal parties, had become more tense amid growing uncertainty. Fresh elections had been called, for 23 September, to play out the charade of installing a new President, following the resignation of the interim Peronist government elected in March: Juan Perón was to be the new head of state. His followers still pretended to show a unified front for the elections; but the old man's following was fragmented and scrapping for a share of his power. However, even journalists had to get on with the job and pay the bills. Polo worried, as did all journalists, and remarked, as did everybody, 'What are we coming to', and like all others expected no answer.

So on that spring morning Polo stepped out on to the pavement. He looked over his shoulder up the street to see if the bus was coming. The street, straight and unusually empty for several blocks, had only one car parked on his side. He crossed to the bus stop to wait for the *colectivo*. He trotted gently. He grabbed the steel pipe that marked the stop, swung around it once and then stood upright again, hitching his camera bag onto his shoulder. He heard the engine start in the car that had been parked just beyond the front door of his building; the car moved towards him. He watched it without registering its movement because it was unimportant.

Five yards away the car stopped; Polo thought there would be a request for assistance to find an address. The half-open back window of the car slid down and a man's face popped out. The face had on it what Polo thought was a smile. It looked familiar; but Polo could not place it. An arm beckoned him.

'Where're you going? Can we give you a lift?' the man with his head out of the window called. As he heard the voice there was a little snap in Polo's memory: it was one of those Peronist faction leaders he had photographed during the previous election campaign. Strange that he should be helpful now. He must want something... He had ignored Polo on the few occasions that their paths had crossed at press conferences or party meetings.

'No, thanks,' Polo said. 'I'm off to work ... to the magazine. I'll take the bus.' He was not in a mood for company; he had to think about the work waiting for him, bills to pay ... and he would rather be alone. He smiled and shook his head.

'Come on,' the man in the car insisted, 'We'll take you... It's a short ride.'

'No, really, thank you ... another time.' Polo smiled.

There was a long pause. The man in the car turned his head slowly to look at someone else on the seat beside him, then back at Polo. 'Get in, damn you.' It was said with clenched teeth, without humour.

Polo winced. Then he found a half smile and muttered, 'Oh, well.'

He crossed in front of the car and saw that the man beside his acquaintance in the back seat was wearing dark glasses. The driver also wore dark glasses. The international disguise of political intrigue, Polo thought with a sigh and an inward smile at what he reckoned was a clever phrase. Polo opened the front door and swung into the seat, too fast to notice that the seat was only the metal frame, draped with green towelling. He went through the frame and hit the floor with a painful bump. Even more painful was the bar at the back of the seat frame which rubbed his spine as he dropped. He was pinned to the floor of the car by his own weight, unable to lift himself without hurting his back again. His light clothes, a thin pair of trousers, a T-shirt and over that a cotton shirt, had not cushioned his fall. He groaned, half-turned his shoulders awkwardly and forced a pale smile with a protesting 'Hey' in his voice, as the door was slammed shut. He felt rather like a schoolboy who comes out of a mauling with a toothless grin which shields the near tears. He grabbed the side bars of the seat frame and tried to lift himself off the floor slightly; but immediately that strained his hands and arms excruciatingly.

His acquaintance called out 'Let's go.' The car started with a lurch, causing Polo more pain in his buttocks and back. When they had crossed the first corner, a newspaper was thrown onto Polo's lap. He tried to grab it with one hand; but it meant releasing his grip on the bars of the seat frame, which put more pressure on his back. It was a copy of the Montoneros' magazine with the doctored group photo under the headline *These are the murderers.* The man in the back seat grinned at the camera from the centre of the page; he was one of the right-wing gang leaders.

'That's yours . . .' said a voice from the back. Until then Polo had felt only apprehension. Now he was afraid. Politics was a game he knew had serious rules; but he had never learned any of them because he did not want to play. The new feeling of fear had only a couple of seconds to speed up the pace of his heart, when four fingers and a thumb gripped the back of his neck and pressed. The pain increased. 'Stop,' he called, and the hand, perhaps unconsciously, reacted to the order, releasing the grip slightly; then the pressure was immediately renewed.

'You gave those bastards the photo. Didn't you?'

'No, I didn't,' Polo coughed, his eyes shut, in pain.

'You were the only photographer at that meeting. They brought you because they trusted you.' Unexpectedly the fierce accusing tone changed to reasoning: 'Don't you know we'll be finished if somebody shows that to the *Viejo* [the Old Man: Perón] . . . if he ever hears of this. . . Has it never even crossed your stupid mind that we could be thrown out of the movement for this?'

The man with the hand on Polo's neck cleared his throat and told the driver: 'Head for Ezeiza.'

The voice came through the hum of semi-consciousness and disbelief; it cut through the whistle in Polo's ears. Ezeiza, next to the airport, was a wooded picnic area which had become a killing ground, a place associated with death since the return of Juan Perón.

'No, wait!' Polo shouted. They remained silent. The muzzle of a gun was pushed in front of his eyes and withdrawn in the same movement, then banged hard behind his ear. Polo opened his mouth wide and heaved a loud 'No...' As tears filled his eyes he yelled 'No! ... Please, oh, please... Why?'

'To whom did you give that photo?' the voice of the man he knew came from the back seat. Polo tried to pull forward and away from the grip of the fingers; but they only tightened on his nape, holding him back. He tried to take a big breath of air into his lungs and choked. The car gained speed along Rivadavia Avenue, heading west. He did not know if they would turn towards Ezeiza later; but they were going in the general direction of the airport. Polo considered which were the fastest roads to get to Ezeiza as if he were an ordinary passenger. Then he hoped for a traffic light, something that would slow them down, maybe let him leap out into the street, or call another motorist. One hand moved stiffly from the seat frame towards the door handle; his body sank to the floor, but the pain now was not as harsh as he had feared; the grip on his neck hurt far more. His hand moved a few inches and no further. The gun that had been jabbing behind his ear was poked firmly into his back and that too was hurting. Would anybody rescue him if he called out? Most certainly not; his captors probably had valid documents to show they were police. He groaned and his voice died in a whimper.

So many men with guns nowadays carried police licences. The guerrillas carried official documents as a rule, which they forged when necessary. The para-official counter-terror groups bragged about their police connections. These included sympathetic police, army, and navy officers who issued the required gun permits, or covered up with good arguments should something go wrong. The officers also supplied full dossiers on the targets sought.

A few days before, Polo had been driven at speed along a busy suburban high street, and his driver, a young man attached to the federal police as an informer, had opened the sun roof of his Peugeot car and fired the full magazine of a Colt .45 into the air. The sound had been thunderous, the repercussions non-existent.

Now his shoulders ached, his back was in agony, his arms were under strain and his legs felt cramped as he had to keep them bent high, his knees almost level with his shoulders. He thought of nothing but his pain and of his fear of the three men. He tried to think of something useful; an influential name to mention; a plea for the sake of his wife and children; but nothing came to mind. He only thought of being pinned down in the seat, trapped.

The car stopped at a red light. 'Don't get it into your head that you are going to shout or leap out. There is no way you can get out, because the door locks from outside. This car belongs to the police: it has been fixed for dumping traitors like you. If you shout, Cacho here will shoot.'

Polo felt comforted by the knowledge of the name of the man behind him: Cacho. It was a nickname; but in the circumstances it was something. He thought, in his desperation and in his struggle to clutch at anything, that it might make communication easier.

'If you don't shout, you have a good chance of staying alive all the way to the Ezeiza woods...'

'And then...' Polo shrieked. He cried, choked on his tears, coughed and his whole body ached. 'But I'm young,' he said and was conscious of sounding ridiculous.

'Eh...' the driver said, shrugging his shoulders and lifting his hands briefly from the wheel, palms up. 'What do you expect? These are difficult times. We can't take these risks and you must understand. We've waited months to come for you...' Somebody let us down; we have to get him out of the way. You gave away Miguel's picture to the Montos...'

Ah, Polo thought, a second name. That's right, he was called Miguel.

'Well, we have to make sure that it does not happen again. Some you win ... some you lose. Today you lose. We lost two men in San Isidro the other day, down by the fishing pier. They were ambushed by the Montos who said they had left them to come to us... Quite unnecessary the way they did them in. More than twenty bullets each. I think that's exaggerating things. And one of our blokes was married, his wife pregnant...' The man at the wheel smiled; Polo thought that he was recalling the dead friend; but it was not that. 'I laid her once, in his bed. Well, he was in Villa Devoto prison; I went to visit her.'

The calm voice, the rational inhumanity sounded so routine. Polo was momentarily comforted by the steady voice. He shut his eyes tight as pain stabbed at the region of his bladder.

'No!' he blared with all the air in his lungs. 'No, let me go!' The force found in his lungs pressed down on his waist and a warm wetness spread over his trousers. He had lost control of himself. He tried to stop the flow but failed to.

From the back seat he heard Cacho, the man with the vice-like fingers, tell Miguel, the man who had been in the photograph: 'This guy's wet himself. C'mon, step on it,' he told the driver.

The driver remarked that it was not unusual for people in this situation to wet their pants.

'Miguel, Cacho...' Polo said as calmly as he could. 'Somebody must have taken that picture from the files. Look, ask the people at the *Popular* paper about my work. Please, they can give you good references. I never took pictures out of any file...'

'That's just what we need... references from the socialist newspaper.' Again, the exchange sounded reasonable, perhaps because everything was absolutely normal; there is no such thing as something socially unconventional on the way to death; there was not a word that sounded mockable, or out of place, nor anything implausible.

The man named Miguel suddenly tapped the driver on the shoulder and the car slowed down. Unbelievably he said, looking at Polo, 'Let's go back to the socialist newspaper. It's by Madero Avenue.' The grip snapped back on Polo's neck, just as he started to relax. The renewed pressure, the mixture of feelings, the apparent hesitation of his captors, became too much. A drain-like noise from his gut, which seemed to twist and unknot, was followed by a rattle which came above the car's acceleration; Polo felt a warm thick paste fill the seat of his tight trousers.

'Jesus, now this bastard has shat himself,' the driver yelled.

Miguel stretched forward and pulled away the Montonero magazine that had been on Polo's lap half covering the wet patch of urine.

'Christ, open the windows.'

'Let's go to Ezeiza,' the driver shouted. 'Let's finish this job. I've got to pay my electricity bill before the office closes at three.'

'No. Let's go down to the *Popular*; then we can go to Ezeiza. But open the window...' Miguel ordered.

The driver reached over and wound down the window. Cacho tightened his grip and Polo let out a yelp.

'Don't try anything or you'll find me keeping your voice between my fingers for good.'

'No,' coughed Polo.

'A shitter like you deserves this.' Cacho squeezed, his eyelids closing over a flicker of a smile.

The driver became impatient. He slammed in the gears one after another, nosed the car through the late morning traffic and found Córdoba Avenue, then sped east, away from Ezeiza towards the port, his foot never off the accelerator. He leant forward and flicked a switch under the dashboard; a police siren wailed from beneath the bonnet and echoed against the tall buildings on both sides of the wide avenue. He swerved past one car; narrowly avoided a crossing van as he dashed through a red light; tyres shrieked as he swerved to miss two pedestrians.

Miguel took a pistol from the seat beside him, put his arm

out of the back window and waved the barrel of the gun from side to side in a signal to all road-users to clear the way. They braked hard several times; but the siren took them through. In what seemed to be only a few minutes they were swerving into Madero Avenue, parallel with the port fence.

'We're going up to check on you. What is it? Fifth floor... eh?'

Polo nodded.

The driver took the car up to Plaza Mazzini, a shaded square flanked at the north and south ends by tall offices and old once-elegant apartment buildings, in one of which was the socialist paper's newsroom; on the east nearest the port and the River Plate was the concrete hulk of the new plant of the conservative newspaper *La Nación*, and to the west was the wide, high-speed Leandro Alem Avenue. The car was driven once around the square, then parked on the street between the *La Nación* building and Plaza Mazzini – named after the Italian revolutionary theorist.

There were a few seconds of silence in which a long sigh by Polo was heard. 'We're leaving him here,' said Miguel. 'I don't want this guy. I'll take his story.' Cacho's hand opened; Polo's head flopped forward.

'OK,' the driver said, in the North American manner, 'So we don't want you.' He tutted. 'Better... I couldn't stand this stink much longer.' He got out of the car and went round the front to Polo's door, which he opened from the outside. 'Get out,' he snapped.

Polo looked up, helpless, pleading for understanding in his humiliation. 'Get out.' As Polo tried to use his numb hands to lift himself out, the driver grabbed his hair and yanked him out. Polo howled as he was lifted by his hair and then thrown face down on the pavement, onto his camera bag. The driver slammed the door shut and ran back to his seat.

The tyres spun under sudden acceleration before they gripped; then the car lurched forward, but stopped. It was reversed the three yards it had travelled and the soiled towelling that had covered the seat frame in which Polo had been trapped was flung out of the window onto the sprawling body.

Polo made no attempt to get up from the pavement, by the yellowish trunk of a large plane tree. The blood throbbed back into his aching legs; his arms felt limp. His body shook with a great shiver, a sob rose in his stomach and coughed out from his throat. He cried loudly, freely, uncontrollably, unaware of the few people passing, staring at him but not stopping. Eventually he sat up. Without lifting himself he moved to the granite kerb stone. He sat there, once again with his legs bent, embraced by his arms, and he put his closed eyes against his knees. He rocked himself slowly and sobbed. He heard somebody say, *pobrecito* (poor thing), and walk on. An old woman, one of the three or four tramps who made Plaza Mazzini their home, limped by, muttering something about, 'Some days are filled with bad luck.'

A police patrol car drew near him and the driver asked brusquely what was the matter.

'I shat myself,' Polo told the policeman, attempting an embarrassed smile.

'*Ay, pobrecito*. It must have been something you ate that has affected your liver. Why don't you go over to the *La Nación* building and ask the foreman if you can have a wash.' The patrol car left.

Polo stared at the building of the newspaper *La Nación* for a long time. There was a small entrance through a temporary pallisade around the site. He considered whether to go there; but decided to walk the five blocks of parking lots and portside avenues back to the news magazine. He wondered about the reception that he might get, arriving in the stench of his own excrement. Then he dismissed the speculation as too distressing. He decided he had to get the photo-files locked forever or purged of every picture he had ever taken, even the fashion pictures. He sobbed at the thought of the work this would mean. There must be thousands of his pictures. He had to do it without saying what had happened.

He unbuttoned his shirt slowly and took it off. He had a T-shirt underneath and the sun was high now, so he would not feel cold. His interminable ordeal had lasted just over one hour. It felt as if it had happened weeks ago. He recalled that at no time in the last hour had he thought of the form of death he might have suffered; nor had his memory brought the image of his wife and children or of what would happen at any time beyond the minute he was living. He realised that this must have been the ultimate trick of the subconscious in the preservation of himself. The prospect was too horrifying; the pain he had endured had been distracting; his fear and humiliation had occupied all of his conscious self.

He stood, his legs weak. He tied the shirt sleeves around his waist so that the shirt covered his backside. The camera bag he held in front, to cover the wet patch which, at its outer edge, was beginning to dry. He walked stiffly, self-consciously, towards the magazine.

The porter slipped a blank envelope under the apartment door. It was eight months later. Some cabinet ministers had changed; many allegiances had, too. Things seemed to be getting more unsettled and times more violent. Polo's wife opened the envelope and read out the handwritten note:

Dear Polo,
Sorry about what we did to you. You must understand, it was an accident. I want to make amends. I have opened a restaurant in Flores and would like to give you a first rate meal. Bring the family. Greetings, Miguel.

An address was written in careful block capitals at the bottom of the page. Before she had put down the note, Polo's curiosity had decided his answer.

He went on Sunday night with his wife and children, unannounced. He walked into a richly decorated, expensive restaurant. The place was dimly lit and a *tango* about the singer's memories of the streets of Buenos Aires in years gone by was playing softly. There were few diners: it was early.

'Polo!' Miguel yelled. 'Welcome.' Polo was embraced; his wife was kissed and her neatly set hair was ruffled into disorder in a gesture of fondness; the children were lifted, kissed, and danced across the polished brick floor. Behind the over-decorated bar, with dark imitation wood panelling, with plastic galleons and shields and autographed pictures of television personalities, was Cacho. He stood at the till, eating *pretzels*. He held each *pretzel* with two fingers and a thumb and snapped them in half; then popped both pieces into his mouth with a stiff lethargic movement. The 'driver' was also behind the bar counter, taking an order from one of three waiters. They waved at Polo, looked at one another with a grin, came out to shake hands and then excused themselves to go back to work. Miguel led the family to a table, excitedly telling Polo and his wife what a happy occasion it was that they should have come. He had only recently finished the decorating and was so anxious to share everything with his friends.

3

BROTHERS' RANSOM

June 1975

There are some stories that journalists dream of being able to cover. Some stories they write about, yet are not there to cover. Once in a while there is a good story they cover but cannot write about. The release of Jorge Born, after nine months as a captive of guerrillas, is my example of a story covered but not told.

On a bright Thursday morning in September 1974, just before the beginning of spring, Jorge and Juan Born, directors of the export-based Bunge & Born corporation, were abducted by guerrillas. The attack, named *Operation Twins*, had been carefully planned and was executed with the mastery gained by political confidence; guerrilla tactics and logistics were in competent hands. One moment the Born brothers and one of their subsidiary company managers were being driven by a chauffeur along a tree-lined residential avenue in La Lucila, on their way into their city office; the next moment there was a policeman who signalled to them to turn into a side street. Behind the policeman were two men in state telephone utility overalls who appeared to be starting some kind of work. As soon as the chauffeur turned the car, the road-block was lifted and the traffic flowed normally. As the chauffeur headed for a street which ran parallel to the avenue, next to the suburban railway line, several more men in overalls got out of a parked car. The chauffeur feared a trap and tried to turn back. The ambushers started shooting. The chauffeur and the subsidiary manager were murdered. Juan and Jorge Born were transferred to waiting cars and disappeared.

The kidnapping was a front page spectacular. Then, like all

news items, it dropped from front to inside pages, where the occasional leak about ransom negotiations was carried. From there it passed after a few weeks into the realm of rumour. The guerrillas set a ransom of 60 million dollars. The sum was unprecedented. The previous high had been 15 million dollars for a United States oil company executive.

'Can we talk somewhere?' the young man who had come into the newsroom asked. I sighed, apprehension in my jerky breath, as I assented. I led him along the narrow passage to the small library. We remained standing. His hair was combed back, a perfumed lotion keeping every strand in place. He was neatly dressed in spotless grey flannels, blue jacket and silk tie; he took care of his appearance both to escape notice in the street, and as an expression of vanity: Italian immigration's legacy to Argentina.

The young man said that he had come to invite me to a press conference called by the Montoneros 'superior command'. The invitation was announced in the tone of declamation; he was not merely a messenger but a herald. It was intriguing, but irritating.

I agreed to go. He gave me a time and a place at which to meet a guide. It was not the first guerrilla press conference I had been invited to, so this time I simply put my hand on my chest and felt my heartbeat accelerate.

On an unexpectedly warm and sunny Friday morning which happened to be a public holiday in June 1975, I went, as arranged, to the *La Biela* bar. It was across a graceful *plaza* from the entrance to the Recoleta Cemetery. The Recoleta – about which Jorge Luis Borges has written poems in an old man's celebration of death – is the repository of the country's illustrious, probably the most expensive real estate in Argentina; which is a piece of useless information that finds its way into every North American news writer's copy. *La Biela* was the place of reunion of the young, upper-middle-class men and women of Buenos Aires, *Porteños*, sympathetic either to the guerrillas or their rivals. The bar was a regular target for bombings, as much for its symbolic value as for its capacity to command press coverage. It was a predictable meeting place.

One third of the floor space of *La Biela* was cordoned off and cleared of tables to allow the builders and decorators to disguise the damage caused by the latest bombing. I took a table nearest the cordon and ordered a cup of coffee. A man sat down with a muttered greeting and asked, 'Who else is coming?' He was a reporter who had recognised me. His question was answered when another journalist joined us; he announced that he was not working on the story because he was our guide.

At the Retiro terminal he bought three tickets to Acassuso. I was more nervous now. I had lived at Acassuso for six years.

The train was crowded with day trippers to the Tigre islands at the end of the line. They made a cheerful, noisy band, but I was unaffected by the modest euphoria of released office workers. I felt drowsy, not only from the late newsroom shift of the night before, but because the anonymity and individuality of sleep is the protective recourse of the subconscious.

On arrival at Acassuso we parted. They got off at the front of the train, nearest the level crossing and the high street. I got out at the back end, where there were a few shops outside the station, none of which I had visited as a customer. I walked past a parked police patrol car and tried to ignore it. When the car was several steps behind me, the voice of one of the four men inside called out, '*Eh ... Che...*' and I froze. 'Don't you say hello any more?' It was a middle-aged sergeant, a man named Ayala, from the 'old guard' of the Buenos Aires province police. He was a likeable, helpful man; we had met when I had reported the theft of my car, and he had been angry and embarrassed because one of his policemen on the night round was suspected. Ayala had gained his last stripe a few months before, when he had been seriously injured trying to disarm a bomb, planted by Montoneros in a public square. He had read about my recent arrest for publishing an interview with guerrillas and was amused by my imprisonment. 'Visiting friends?' he asked. I nodded.

One hundred yards away, my travelling companions were

39

looking my way. When we met again I was questioned briefly about my encounter. There was no suspicion in the guide's questions, only mild curiosity. We trusted one another over the political abyss between us.

We walked along a street named *Libertad,* though I only thought of the irony in the name some hours later. We reached a house with a low brick wall, topped with a tight wooden palisade that blocked the front garden from view. It was a grey flat-roofed two-storey house, perhaps built 30 years before – old in this suburb – for the affluent tasteless. It had large picture windows with the blinds down, and a long concrete balcony running the length of the top floor. The area was one of comfortable houses with gardens, homes of the rising middle class.

The ring of the doorbell was answered by an attractive young woman wearing a maid's uniform: black cotton blouse and skirt, short white starched apron, starched collar and cuffs. She greeted our guide with recognition in her smile and showed us into the house. I stared at her back as she led us in: she really was good-looking. The tiny front hall led into a combined lounge and dining room, lit only by artificial light; the blinds to the street and back garden were down. The house smelled of floor polish and dampness. I wondered if the guerrillas had rented the house and remarked to the guide: 'Headquarters...? Looks sufficiently neglected.' He was not amused. I felt a little afraid; what if they got nasty or if police came? A selection of the most infantile and inadequate explanations for my presence there came to mind: an anonymous caller told me there might be something interesting for me here... A relative lives nearby, and as I passed somebody I know waved me in...

My flesh soon covered in goose pimples at the stupidity of such thoughts. If police came the guerrillas would use us as shields. We would go down first; no need to bother with excuses. They would never be used.

Fellow reporters became recognisable in the dim light. They sat in the lounge, as in a hospital waiting room, in four compact rows of seats with their backs to the front of the house and facing a shiny veneer table. The lounge looked small because of a large glass cabinet and a sideboard against two of the three walls behind the table. Our guide walked ahead of us to greet some friends who came through a door from an inner room. Apart from the maid there were no other women among the guerrillas. The men were all smartly dressed, most of them wearing suits and ties. The two of us who had just arrived were frisked by a young man with a cadaverous face, who uttered not a greeting nor a request to proceed as his open hands moved rapidly over our bodies. He reminded me of a police clerk who had taken my finger prints after arrest one night. Once released from the searcher's contempt, I looked at the back of a short stocky man who was wolfing morsels from a platter placed on a large dark wood sideboard running the length of one lounge wall. Two .45 pistols, a machinegun, and several small objects which must have been grenades lay on the table near the plate.

'Paco?' I enquired cautiously of the stocky back. A former journalist chum, Francisco Urondo, turned to face me, holding out the platter full of warm *empanadas* (pasties) and a glass of white wine. When our eyes met, he put down glass and plate, wiped his mouth with the back of his hand and without a word we embraced, held one another at arms' length and smiled in silence.

'I haven't seen you for ages,' I said.

'Orders,' he said, by way of explanation. We smiled and shrugged. He pushed away the glass of wine he had been about to give me and took a larger glass and filled it. 'I know my friends' bad habits,' he said with a broad grin. He shoved one *empanada* into my mouth and another into my free hand. I chewed awkwardly. A silly cloud of tears welled up behind my eyes, then vanished with a blink. Paco, in his mid-forties, had become an officer with the guerrillas. Before that he had been a senior member of the neo-Marxist Revolutionary Armed Forces which had been absorbed by Montoneros. His militancy had only become known to the public in February 1973 when police arrested him in a raid on a cottage outside Buenos Aires. He had been reported by a gardener who had seen a rifle in the house. Paco had been freed by the Peronist government's amnesty in May 1973 and had rejoined his group. His fame, however, sprung from his poetry. He was one of Argentina's best poets.

Paco motioned to the seats. 'We're starting soon. Find a chair.' I asked if we could talk later, but he shook his head.

I made my way around the tripods, recording equipment and cameras of a television crew who were either German or Swedish. I did not ask. Foreigners were invited because the Montoneros feared that local crews would betray the meeting to the police. The cameras worried me. I felt the lightness of fear, when the blood is thin and fingertips lose some of the sense of touch.

A man checked the faces present. Another stood in front of us with a stack of multicoloured plastic-covered folders. This was sophistication: the guerrillas handing out press kits. The first leaf, a type-written carbon copy, informed us that this was a press conference; it would last approximately one hour; it would be addressed by the Montoneros commander, Mario Eduardo Firmenich; members of the press had to sit still and in silence, with eyes front. As if on cue, a few of us swung in our seats and looked behind towards the entrance. It was the sum of our defiance. The folder had no instructions on what to do in case of a police raid. There was a detailed account of the abduction of the Born brothers accompanied by maps of the ambush; there were photographs of the two men in captivity and a collection of statements on recent military action by Montoneros. Possession of such papers is what journalistic egos are made of.

We had hardly been given time to peruse the waiting-room literature when we heard the front door being opened. There were excited voices, formal and friendly greetings. Firmenich came in, dressed in smart trousers, jacket and tie. He carried a briefcase; I speculated on its contents and decided that they had to be an automatic pistol and half a dozen hand grenades; or else that morning's newspaper, two ham sandwiches, a cold *tortilla* oozing oil into its brown paper wrapping, and an orange. He walked quickly through the lounge to what must have been the kitchen. Minutes later he entered the dining-room by a door at the corner between the sideboard and the glass cabinet, wearing an open short-sleeved shirt and dungarees. He sat down on the only chair placed by the dining table and greeted his audience.

Firmenich, descended from Yugoslav immigrants, was the supreme commander of Montoneros. He had been among the founders, whose political apprenticeship had varied. Most of the twelve young men and women who (at the end of May 1969) had kidnapped and later murdered a former president of Argentina, had their origins in right-wing nationalism; their guidebooks not *Das Kapital* but the Scriptures. Some of those in that first dozen had been killed in gunbattles, some had joined other factions. Firmenich had inherited the leadership.

The guerrilla chief spoke with controlled excitement. The press conference had been called because it was Argentina's Flag Day and the second anniversary of Juan Perón's return to Argentina from exile in Spain. The 'imprisonment' of the Born brothers was proof that 'we are now a force to be reckoned with, a political organisation which cannot be ignored'. His preoccupation seemed to be with not being ignored. He was the chief. He had started as a bank robber, a jewel thief, stealing watches to use their mechanism in bombs.

Some day somebody was going to make a film about his life, just as they had recently done with the 1920s story of the East European anarchist immigrants in Patagonia. He would be sketched as a popular hero, dedicated, committed, loved by his men, passionate about many women. Before long, the members of the Institutes of Latin American Studies at universities in the United States and Europe would be writing theses about this man we were hearing. There would be a professor somewhere describing him as a precursor in 'Non-Marxist Dialectics within the Framework of Nationalist Revolutionary Concepts'. You could count on professors to find enough evidence for something daft about Firmenich.

I enjoyed my own train of thought.

Firmenich generously returned my smile and I realised that I was grinning at him.

While my mind had wandered Firmenich had opened the meeting to a brief discussion. He denied that he was a Marxist-Leninist; he had not read either; he was a Socialist Nationalist.

Then he summed up: 'The cost of this war has been high; the cost to individuals is regrettable... Some fool the other day published a list of how many police were killed and how many of our combatants had died. They were all in the same list ... I don't know who wants to keep that kind of list; I think it is ridiculous and quite out of place.' I sat up with a jerk; I had compiled that list. But I lacked the courage to enter an argument.

Firmenich lifted a hand and said that he wanted to tell us something special. 'While I tell you I'd like to shake hands with you because I really must go.' He grinned, then moved to the front row of seats and we stood; it was natural to stand, he was the authority. In Argentina, everybody stands before authority. He shook hands. 'In a few minutes Mr Jorge Born will be brought here. We are presenting him to the press; he will be released today.'

We all looked at one another in unbelieving excitement, in nervous anticipation. This was going to be our big day after all. As Firmenich shook my hand I said, 'That list you said some fool had ... Well, I'm the fool who makes it.'

'Wrong,' Firmenich snapped. 'We make it; you compile it.' He thought his crack was amusing and I obediently laughed. Then he smiled, gripped my hand harder, patted the back of my neck: 'No hard feelings; it's an interesting job you've done.' He moved on to greet others.

'How much did you get for Born?' somebody asked. Firmenich smiled back and his smugness seemed to form a cloud around him, 'What we set out to get: 60 million dollars.'

We wanted to know where the money was. I found myself wondering if our presence entitled us to a small cut, but attributed such a peregrine thought to the large quantity of white wine with which I had been supplied by Paco. Guerrillas usually offered wine at press conferences. They did this as a sign of hospitality and, less noticeably, as a symbol of

44

their self-confidence and of the calm and lack of urgency with which they could entertain their guests. For me, the light golden liquid was not an *apéritif* but an elixir which edged me to the border between cold sobriety and the light jollity of early inebriation, when nerves are blunted to the sensation of danger.

Firmenich would not say if the money was in the country or abroad, which seemed a very reasonable reply; people do not go around shouting their bank account number.

Somebody called, 'There he comes!' Stepping carefully down a set of stone stairs with no hand rail, peering through dark glasses with some difficulty, Jorge Born arrived. It seemed simple; he looked quite ordinary; it was not clear to me what I expected to see. A man had to be different to the rest of his species after nine months in captivity.

We searched for the freak in the appearance of Jorge Born. It was not there. His captors addressed him in soft voices; solicitously they asked if he was well, if he needed help to walk, if he would like to sit down. He was led to the dining room, where he leaned with his back against the sideboard, his hands in the pockets of his grey-blue jacket. The journalists crowded around him, then stepped away as the German – or Swedish – television crew switched on the lights and focused their cameras. Born stared at the camera, stunned by the brightness of the lights, by the uncertainty of the situation and by the crowd of people – even though his guards had warned him to expect them. Finally the lights went out. It was exciting to be by him; he was worth 60 million dollars. I felt the pride of professional achievement.

Where was his brother Juan? A guerrilla broke in with the manner of a diligent theatrical agent, concerned that his charge might blunder: Mr Juan Born had been released some months ago. I asked for a date. 'One loses track of dates,' Born said. The best I was offered were guesses. 'December, or January, or maybe April...'

I wondered how they could have freed a man held captive and not know when; but in my impotence shrugged away the doubt. A reporter admired Born's jacket. It was a good fit.

Born agreed. He supposed that his captors could afford it. There was laughter; Born warmed to the people around him. It was remarked that he had a good haircut; he said that his hair had always been kept short. He remarked that he had been brought to this house in a car only a few days before.

One of his captors whispered to him: 'We are taking you out now, Mr Born. We are handing you over to these journalists who will be responsible for your safe return.' There was a sense of nervousness among the reporters: apprehension that this meeting had not ended with the profitable acquaintance of Mr Born. In the silence, the withdrawal from further contact became perceptible squirming.

Paco called out, 'We want two journalists to accompany Mr Born, just two.' There was no explanation as to where he was going and none was requested.

Boldness, professional vanity and curiosity took over: this was a unique opportunity for a reporter. 'I'll go.' Someone else volunteered, perhaps for the same reasons. After that several others offered to go; but it was only a gesture made in the security of its rejection. They were appalled by my conceit and the extent of my apparent complicity.

People got ready to go. Things were being packed; chairs pushed around; the camera tripod folded. A guerrilla held several press kits aloft and asked loudly who could take them to the establishment newspapers *La Prensa, La Nación* and *La Razón.* He cajoled when his appeal met with silence and with heads that turned to seek conversation under the guise of distraction. He found two carriers.

There was a sense of urgency in the room. I saw Firmenich leave, his briefcase in his left hand. He shook hands with his officers and waved to us. Then he shook hands with Jorge Born, saying *'Buenas tardes.'* Born muttered a reply. Firmenich wore a neatly pressed grey suit: three changes in the course of a couple of hours. Somebody rushed down the stairs and announced that he had called the office of the men who had negotiated for Born's release. They had been advised that he should be met near the level crossing at Acassuso station. It did not seem to me a convenient arrangement. I asked a colleague to take my press kit. Born was given a new set of dark glasses, with cotton wool pads on the inside. He was asked politely if he would not mind wearing them.

Two machine-guns made their appearance, aimed at the ceiling, held with the butt on the men's shoulders. One of the guerrillas answered a question about our own safety by saying that they had removed the mouthpiece from the telephone. I remembered that I had not asked who owned the house: Who was in it? How had they got the house? Was it rented? Were the occupants captives or allies? They did not bother to answer. They were not going to tell me.

There was a shout from the door. 'Come on, the two who are travelling with Mr Born.' Paco came from the kitchen and half raised a hand in a signal to me. I stopped on my way to the door and he came over, squeezed my elbow gently and smiled.

'Goodbye; there does not seem much time for a decent chat any more . . .' He chuckled; his hands rose slowly as his arms opened and we gripped one another in a gentle embrace. I nodded a greeting and left him.*

The other journalist and I were marched up to either side of Jorge Born and, like school children harassed by an impatient teacher, were grabbed firmly by the shoulders and pushed until we were standing facing the closed front door. A car started outside and the engine revved. The front door was opened; the bright afternoon sun invaded the front hall. The car reversed up to the front door through open garden gates; the car doors opened, front and back, the driver and his mate nodded.

We were told to help Mr Born into the back seat. 'Keep your eyes closed, Mr Born.' We got into the car, one on each side of Born. 'Keep your eyes closed.' I kept them open; though I glanced at Born to make sure his were well covered and he would not see that mine were open.

The car lurched forward, bumped over the pavement and swung into the street heading towards the station. A wet patch on the smooth cobbles made it slip and swerve; but the avenue

* Francisco Urondo died in a gunbattle in Mendoza in June 1976.

was almost empty and there was no danger in the skid. We stopped at the lights, then turned into the street which led to the station. At the first corner, one block from the railway line, the car stopped.

They were leaving us. 'Just before you go: the two gentlemen will help you out and face you towards the station. You have to walk six paces; do not look back. After that you can take off your glasses,' the driver said.

There was a parting call with an unkind sneer. 'Goodbye, Mr Born. Good luck.' Born raised an arm and acknowledged. We heard two doors slam and I turned to look, only to see the car vanish down the side street.

'What a lovely afternoon', Born said. We introduced ourselves. We asked if he was feeling well, if he wanted to stop for a cup of coffee or a drink. He said he wanted to go home. He was soft-spoken, calm-voiced and a little uncertain of us and of our intentions. There was nobody on the street; two people crossed at the corner, but they were only a blur.

We walked towards the station, crossed the tracks, strolled along the platform and down to the street, to wait for the car. We wondered who would come. There was a possibility that the telephone had been tapped and that the police would pick us up. Which could mean a long time inside for us. Born asked if we could walk about; it was good to be able to walk a distance more than the length of a tiny room. His legs seemed to shiver, as do those of a convalescent after a long illness. He asked permission to walk, to turn back, to stop. Nine months of being bullied and commanded had created that habit.

His quarters had been cramped. His brother had broken down and his early release had been negotiated. Born would not explain. He had done exercises to keep fit, but he was not fit; the words came between long pauses for thought and formulation of sentences. He had only recently learned that his friend and junior executive had been murdered when they were ambushed. Born had suffered the pain of loss for many days.

Jorge Born was evasive about the ransom. He had taken part in the negotiations, but did not know the full extent of the arrangements. Sixty million dollars was a lot of money; one third of the national defence budget for the preceding year, Born estimated. His businessman's mind was grinding slowly into gear. The details and figures were missing – they would come in time – but the resort to comparison of volumes was there. He asked about our work and our papers, but our answers did not register; his thoughts were probably at his home, or in some corner of hatred in his mind, or perhaps already in his office. He was disciplined in his conversation and manner; there seemed no sense in a breakdown, there was time for that. Feelings still had to be controlled. By sparing us from any scenes he became very likeable, extremely reasonable. He said that it would be lovely to be home again. The conversation moved, faltering, to the good winter weather; the street with its huge trees on both pavements; the gardens beyond the pavement in front; the lengthening of the days. We speculated about how long it would take his people to get to the station. His voice was slow, but in all his remarks there was the mild surprise of an inexperienced tourist, an educated tourist, of course. He was a little puzzled by everything around him.

It was a strange gathering. Two journalists chatting with a kidnap victim and apparently bereft of questions. We wondered how much longer it would take. I tried to formulate a good question, but could think of nothing. And there was little I wanted to know that could be told in a newspaper. It was of no concern to readers whose personal problems precluded political human interest stories. I could have asked him what were his washing and toilet facilities; or what he had read and which books he planned to read in the near future; what thoughts, in detail, comforted him, and which alarmed him. But I dared not ask him. So we chatted, like three men caught for a prolonged wait in a bus queue.

Two cars, each with only the driver inside, approached at high speed. On seeing the three men on the pavement, the drivers stopped on the other side of the street. Jorge Born stepped ahead and with voice raised introduced us. He asked that we be given a lift into town. Born answered our farewell greeting and entered one car; we were shown to the other. We had been parted from our big story.

Our driver, a young fair-haired man, was friendly in his conversation, but guarded in his answers. He knew our by-lines, asked about our work, how the press was doing in these troubled times. He wondered how we came to be with Born. Our replies did not seem satisfactory. He had been involved in the negotiations for Born's release and said that during months of contacts he had learned how to talk with his chief's captors. There was little respect for them in his voice; but no anger either. This had been a straight business negotiation in which he had been on the losing side.

He left us on Basavilbaso Street, near Retiro station. There I parted with my colleague, exchanging only a few sentences about the story. I was a little distressed at my lack of emotion about the day's events: no alarm, no concern, no fear. All those things needed time to grow, with time to imagine the consequences. I phoned my wife and then walked the twelve blocks to recover my press kit and back to the paper. I had two double whiskies and a sandwich and then wandered nervously among the desks. The frustrating thing about journalism is that often you know less about a story for being at the centre of it. And I knew no more about Born and the Montoneros than I had known that morning when I had caught the train to my meeting at *La Biela*.

'Better make it a straight report as if it had come in from an agency. No first person anywhere. You've been inside a couple of times and you are facing trial on criminal charges. Neither you nor the paper can take much more.'

Somebody said, 'Pity, anywhere else you might get something like a Pulitzer...'

'Hah,' somebody retorted. 'Here it'll be a bullet, sir.' It caused a few smiles.

We ran the story as if nobody from the paper had been at the press conference. *La Prensa*, which had not been there, used the press kit to full advantage and gave the story a good display, with illustrations. *La Prensa* was taken to court charged with aiding subversion and conspiracy, but won the case and the right to publish. The court's decision was used by my lawyers when my case came up for trial. But that is another story.

4

A MATTER OF FEAR

October 1975

The car coasted to the curb, moving apace with my steps on the pavement. It nosed ahead slowly. Into the vision line of the corner of one eye moved the bonnet; then the brilliance of the windshield came into view. A glance around brought the sight of the small dark hole of the muzzle of a gun resting on the window frame, aimed at me...

Knees reacted first; they did not bend properly. Guilt, due to the existence of a follower, gave rise to the feeling, the certainty, that each awkward step was as noticeable as the impeded gait of a severely handicapped person. My feet trod with short hurried steps on a cushion of air, hesitant whether to touch the ground, to run or slow down, without a suitable order from me. The men in the car were watching me ... The man at the wheel called out something about my beard and added a remark that ended in an oath.

I began to turn my head, slowly, stiffly.

The car drove away. It was not me they wanted this time.

It was not much more than an instant. There were other, longer, more frightening episodes; but none so acute.

An image of fear is never lost. It is merely filed away, for haunting embarrassing recall ... at the pass of a car. We all have, perhaps, at least one personal image of fear. This one is with me, from Buenos Aires, where my fear starts, to London, from Madrid to Managua. Terror is paralysing; hysteria, embarrassing; fear, humiliating. The two former are incidental and fade; fear is a constant companion.

When did this fear begin? In 1971, after an article published in the Buenos Aires newspaper described the rape of a girl, a guerrilla accomplice, in a toilet by one of her guards. The details were supplied by two lawyers, verbatim from her statement to the judge. The article was not signed; but word got around that I had written it – probably among lawyers defending political prisoners.

A man who said he was the girl's boyfriend, but somehow had the looks of a policeman, called on me in the newsroom. He sat by my desk at the *Buenos Aires Herald* all evening and read magazines, but offered little information. He left me wondering. After that there was a small white Fiat car waiting for me late at night at the station when I got out of the train. The car followed me home, or part of the way home, which was only a four-minute walk from the station, Acassuso, a dormitory on the northern riverside.

The car was there with me. Sometimes only once a week, sometimes every night of the week. As a precaution, I took taxis from the station and the cabbies thought me mad, until they got accustomed to my madness, and to the low fare they collected.

If there were no cabs at the station and the white Fiat was there, I took the long way round, up to Santa Fe Avenue, which was better lit, and where tired beaten prostitutes, ageing in the dark and hiding in the day, picked up wretched, bad-tempered motorists and insatiable truck drivers.

After a few days the women began to greet me; they smiled and asked if I had been working hard, and I said, 'Not so bad, and you?' My question sounded quite reasonable and they told me if custom was good or bad. The weather, strikes, the mid-month budget restraints were some of the reasons why fewer motorists might stop for the brief copulation service offered. I felt very much alone on nights when they were all out at work, although I knew they were there because they left plastic shopping bags on garden fences for their friends to notice.

One night the women disappeared for good. In the Odeón café, at the corner in front of the station, the men at the bar said a police corporal at the San Isidro precinct had been squeezing the women for money for some time. On a recent occasion he had become too rough in his demands and had broken one woman's arm.

It was the kind of story that I could not write; hint at possibly, but hints were wasted because people would ask, 'Why bother? Everybody knows that such things go on.' The bravado spent on a daring, but sneaky, hint was useless, and I could not summon the courage for the whole story.

The walk home became lonelier after that. I kept looking back over my shoulder as I walked. I greeted the night-watchman at the San Isidro fire station, hoping that his awareness of my passage would be of some protection. It could not be, of course. But it was a comfort to hear a voice return a greeting at 3 a.m., on the way home.

There were many articles in which I dared myself to make brief references to political anomalies – then I fretted about the reactions to the publication. It was a stupid, not a vicious, circle in which I compelled myself to report and then waited in terror for the outcome. What is more, it was an exhausting exercise which achieved very little. A naval captain, secretary to the force's commander, wrote to me one day denying that naval intelligence had a dossier which linked me with guerrillas. 'If you have a clear conscience, you have nothing to fear,' the officer's letter said. Of course I do not have a clear conscience. Mine has always been quite murky, clouded by the timidity of the small man who dreams of great acts of courage but thinks that even the smallest step out of line will bring dire consequences.

Always walk along the pavement facing the oncoming traffic, was the advice given in political circles. What for? I asked. So that you at least have an idea which car the bullet came from, was the caution with a smile. Such advice was given seriously and followed earnestly in Buenos Aires. But I told myself that my identity documents were in order and that I was guilty of nothing; so why would anybody have cause to touch me? Then, however, a conscious whisper to my neurosis headquarters said that I had been in some places, talked to some kinds of people ... There were friends to remind me that I had been places ... and it was felt that having been places, such as guerrilla press conferences and to the offices of undesirable politicians, and written for disreputable magazines whose pages harboured stories by extremists or homosexuals, was not only a crime, but a risk that only a fool would take.

Political conflict took more lives and the neurosis convinced us all, friends, people in business, politicians and the very ordinary man next door, that our telephones were being bugged, by the government, by the police, by the guerrillas, depending which side we were against.

A one-legged schoolteacher I had been acquainted with some years before, but whom I had not seen for many months, answered my greeting one day in the centre of Buenos Aires with a controlled wave of the hand. Controlled meant that it should not be seen too far away and therefore did not rise above his waist. I stopped him anyway and he smiled stiffly, a greeting which seemed to tell my boundless egocentricity that he thought I was important. That made me feel good.

The good feeling slipped away, however when he mumbled, 'Well, yes... I do read your articles. You are sticking your neck out... Well, yes... I don't think I should stand by you too long... People say you are going to be shot...' He hailed a taxi and in spite of the usual encumbrance that was his artificial leg, he quickly negotiated the traffic, crossed the street, and got into the car.

It had, therefore, not been a smile of admiring recognition: it had been a wince of precaution. I had a need to laugh at the incident, joke about it and tell friends, trying to provoke their laughter, as the only proof that the man's remark was not true. Months later I found out that it was.

After the encounter I began to listen for every car that slowed down outside the house; to wait for a knock at the door in the early hours which would tell me they had come.

Burned cars littered the sides of the wide, at nights lonely, highways leading out of Buenos Aires. Thieves had put them there, after using them or stripping them. The carcass that was left made the job of investigators quite difficult.

Good ideas are always copied. On many a morning, the smouldering ruin of a car, often more than one car, fast new models, not stripped of parts by thieves, were to be found on rubbish dumps or by the side of roads. Usually shanties, where people feared to walk at night, as if the poor did not have enough troubles without this new one, were chosen for a dump.

In the boot of the car, or in what had once been a back seat, there always were one, maybe two, charred remnants of human bodies. The stumps of limbs were tied with wire or chain which had been in part melted and twisted by the heat of the blaze, or were imbedded in the charcoal crust that had once been human flesh. They were to be found at dawn beside the branch roads of the Pan American Highway; on the *quema*, the municipal rubbish dump outside Villa Martelli; or in the woods near the Buenos Aires international airport at Ezeiza. It was only at first light that each case was discovered; the fire in the dark had been passed by, ignored by any motorists in the night who preferred not to venture off the road; police at night did not answer a caller's alarm.

After the first few discoveries of bodies disposed of in this manner, there were official statements of attempts at identification from what was left of the victims' dentures. Soon the explanations were quietly abandoned and none were demanded. The extremes of all persuasions, from guerrillas to government-sheltered paramilitary groups or private armies employed by trade union bosses or businessmen, agreed on the method to get rid of their captives, their traitors and informers, the bodies of those who had died under torture or of those summarily executed in the name of some savage cause.

We took photographs from close up when police allowed photographers near the cars, or from a distance when they did not.

One very hot morning in January, after hearing the early

news on the radio, I drove a borrowed car to a place in the woods near the airport. A freelance cremation had taken place there the night before. Two policemen with machine-guns hanging by shoulder straps were near a car, now a rust-coloured scrap on the hubs of its wheels. The two men were frightened, not of the charred bits but of the fantasies that the mind made of them, here, in this beautiful lonely spot, where the breeze sang a mournful tune in the trees, and on Sundays families stopped for picnics.

The 'mess' (*el lio*), as one policeman later referred to what had once been a body, was out of the gutted car. A wisp of smoke rose from a smouldering cable under the half open bonnet. The whole mass of metal was still warm, radiating a heat that was suddenly comfortable in that chill and shadowy place at the start of a very hot summer day. The body was on a stretcher, without a cover, waiting for a medical officer to wave it away to a crematorium where the job could be finished.

As I went close, the two men, shivering from their own nervous strain at being stationed there since the first grey light, more than from the strange chill, aimed their guns at me and ordered that I should stop at about six paces from the stretcher. I was standing in the ashes of burned grass in a wide scorched circle around the car. The leaves of the trees in a cluster fifteen yards away were burned brown and, higher up, wilted right to the top of the tallest eucalyptus. (I am worried that my memory no longer holds a good picture of that place, a man-made wood, fifteen miles from the centre of Buenos Aires, 500 yards from the speedway to the airport. It had groups of casuarina trees and eucalyptus rising out of the long grass, with cedars and poplars adding shade. It had beauty at a distance. But Sunday crowds, from the road and from the nearby public swimming-baths and sports-grounds, littered it with empty bottles, old cans, knotted contraceptives, and newspaper used for emergencies in place of toilet paper. But a description escapes me for the wooded garden-like charm mixed with the residue of urban squalor.)

I told the police that I was a journalist and wanted to have a look. I still smoked then and had a packet of cigarettes. I lit one and offered the packet, from six paces, 'Or have you had enough smoke,' I cracked. Why do the crudest remarks come to mind always at times that demand the caution of solemnity, or is it only to my mind? 'Don't laugh,' I was scolded. 'Can't you see how he is, poor thing (*pobrecito*).' I was a little rattled that they should refer to it as 'him'. 'You mustn't laugh, because you never know what might happen to you,' one policeman said. 'You never know who he might have been.' I shivered too. 'He must have been involved,' I said, trying to gain their trust, though a little disgusted at myself for currying favour with the two policemen by appearing to discuss the former person from what might have been described as their angle. 'You never know what people get involved in. That's why one has to be careful nowadays,' came one policeman's reply. 'In the old days my father kept me under close scrutiny and I respected him,' he said, assuming that the dead person was young. One of the men came towards me to take the cigarette that I was still offering. As he put it to his lips, he shivered again, as a man does after·urinating. He said that I should not go nearer. Those were his orders. I said that I just wanted a quick look and then I would go away. He looked around and his mate nodded approval. He said I had two minutes and no more.

I walked to the stretcher and whistled softly, more to give an appearance of nonchalance and confidence than from anything I really felt.

'Suntanned, isn't he?' said one policeman and chuckled. The other tutted.

There was no body. It was a burned crust. The arms and legs and head had shrunk to maybe about two-thirds of their size. They looked like stumps on a gingerbread man, was my only irrelevant thought. I wanted to know what was left of the human flesh and I bent over the bundle, but could only smell a strong sweet odour of roasted meat. It was, remotely, the smell of barbecued beef, but a little off. It was a sweetish smell and I was surprised that I was not revolted by it. Arthur Koestler, in 'Spanish Testament', described the smell of burning human bodies as one that was particularly identifiable, as have many reporters and foreign correspondents covering conflicts. But the smell's horror must be more in the mind. I looked at the skull – *Skol, prosit, chin chin, salud*, I thought – to see if it was burst, as I had been told by a wag that the top of skulls popped with the heat; but there was no evidence of a burst that I could see, and only the remote shape of the front of a head was noticeable.

I walked round to the side of the bundle and bent over it. I glanced up, without lifting my head, to see if the policemen were keeping watch on me. I thought their eyes seemed askance but still I wanted to touch the remains. After what felt like hours of hesitation, bent over the body, I made up my mind and lashed out with my foot. The kick was too hard and I froze almost on contact. The shoe had pushed the crust in roughly below what might have been the rib cage. My toe cap slid from what might have been a bone, or just a hard burned bit which resisted the blow, to enter a hard-surfaced softer area which fell away in the shape of a toe-cap, like soft plaster on a wall. Inside, there was a reddish-yellow looking tissue, quite dry at first, but then an oily, transparent matter began to ooze. That had been a human being.

One policeman rushed to me, gripped me by the shoulder and pulled me straight, pushing me away. He shouted at me for betraying his confidence; yelling, near screaming, at me for my savagery. The other man, behind him, shouted repeatedly, 'Now, let him have it. Let him have it...' The man who grabbed me was near shock, his panic partly caused by concern that he would be in trouble when the forensic doctor came. He shouted that I should go away, threatened to arrest me and then said I deserved to be shot. The other man called out, 'Yes, yes, let him have it ... Step aside, I'll shoot him.' I yelled, 'Don't shoot...' with my free hand in the air in automatic surrender. The other hand was being squeezed by the policeman, a man shorter than I but thick set. After that I do not know what he shouted; but I seem to remember many oaths and threats. And I could only squeal in a shrieky voice 'Don't shoot.' Finally he pushed me away and I stumbled into the burned grass and fell, coughing and spluttering as I raised a cloud of ash, calling in tears, 'Don't shoot...' I crawled to the rim of the ashes and stood shakily in the grass. I heard a safety catch smack and swung round screaming, pleading, tears clouding the two blue uniforms in front of me. 'Go away,' the man who had held me yelled.

I stumbled, my knees missing, my buttocks tight to counter the loosening of my bowels even though my stomach felt snarled like a wrung floor mop. For some reason I tried to clean my shoe in the grass by the car. I got into the car and started the engine never looking back, or even ahead for that matter, because later I could not remember turning the car round onto the road. When I looked up, eventually, into the mirror, I saw my face streaked with dried tears and the ash which had been on my hands. I drove the first three miles on the way home at no more than five miles an hour, hoping that the traffic police would not stop me because I would have to explain the mess my clothes were in. Police would demand an explanation for my appearance. There was no telling, but there was a chance to guess quite accurately, what the policemen back in the field might do if we met again.

It was the abduction of an old lawyer, aged 67, a Trotskyist of no great spark and the elder brother of a former president, that shattered all vestige of calm inside me. It was spring in Buenos Aires and the weather was becoming warm and wonderful. There had been ninety political murders in three months.

The dead ranged from children aged four months to men of nearly 70, caught in the violent dispute for political succession to the former strongman's leadership.

It was a Friday afternoon and I was planning to take an early cut from the paper, to get to a garden cocktail-party near home. The formula was one of comfort, spring, Friday and a garden party and it made the very idea of ninety political murders unreal, something that I could not, rather, would not, have happening around me.

The wires flashed the report of his abduction at about 3 p.m., the urgency of the 'ping, ping, ping' bearing the same excitement for murder as for soccer results. The domestic agency had monitored the Federal Police radio frequency as it was being reported to headquarters. The first flash announced that the old man's flat had been raided by unidentified armed men. The second flash added the useless information that they had been at lunch inside the flat when the door to their apartment was almost thrown off its hinges by the raiders. The third flash said that the old man had been shot and wounded as he was dragged down four flights of stairs and the next cable said that the son-in-law, a 25-year-old engineer, had been shot dead on the pavement while trying to pull the old man away from his captors.

The old man's wife had been hit several times with the butt of a gun and knocked out as she too had joined the struggle; the only one who could still stand at the end of the attack was their daughter, by then a widow.

The old lawyer had been bundled into a car waiting at the door of the apartment building, while armed men had taken position behind two large plane trees on the opposite pavement. Two cars, one at each end of the block, closed the street to all traffic. None of the three cars had licence plates. Uniformed members of the Federal Police, posted two blocks away, had not been called or had stayed away from the street of the raid.

As the story took shape, a freelance photographer called the paper and asked if I would join him in a spot check in the Ezeiza woods in case the story ended there. I said I preferred not to; I argued that I was busy; I could not leave the paper at that time; I had a party that night. As I put the telephone down, our own photographer came from the wireroom wondering aloud if we should go to Ezeiza. Curiosity took over. Guilt, pride and curiosity, really. We called the freelance, who had a van, and he came to fetch us.

As the van nosed through the afternoon traffic to get to the Avenida Riccieri which led to the airport, we talked about the attack with what evidence we had. The old man had been a lawyer for guerrillas, everybody knew that. Some time later it would be learned that he had kept detailed records on their lives and deaths. He had stored the records in a bank's safe deposit which had been accidentally searched by investigators following a robbery. One folder revealed the account by an imprisoned guerrilla who had witnessed how some of his comrades had been pushed to their deaths out of a helicopter in Tucumán province, in revenge for the murder by guerrillas of several army officers.

The van reached the open speedway to the airport and the driver put his foot down. We muttered about the old man's abduction and how we would have to search the woods and the fields when we arrived at the clover-shaped bridge before the airport, which was the area where most bodies had been found. We had little apprehension about the scene we would find or whether the police would let us reach it. The freelance, who was driving, asked us how we had got the news, an inevitable question in the trade. He said that he had been called while he was sitting in the toilet reading a novel. So the subject moved to our choice of literature for the toilet and thereafter the conversation was much livelier.

A police prowl car with its siren at full scream overtook us but none of the four uniformed men spent a glance our way. Our driver said that he would stay as short a time as possible because he wanted to get to the agencies to sell the picture for the European morning papers. If he moved fast, he could get a good deal. It was all so natural and so reasonable. It was a job.

We were among the first to arrive. The patrol car that had overtaken us had left the road in a cloud of dust and we followed it beyond some trees. They knew where to go. 'They've probably been tipped off by the guys who took him,' our driver said.

There was no bar to our approach to the body and the two photographers with me went to work before they could be stopped. The two policemen nearest to the body stepped back to be out of the picture. Several plainclothesmen stood by two cars that had no marks and no plates, but they did nothing to help the men in uniform and nothing to stop us. As a reporter, there was hardly any work for me except to ask how long the body had been there and other routine questions. It was nearly two hours since the first flash in the wire room.

The body lay in shallow grass, the blades still with warm blood on them, and the clumps of taller weeds still working themselves upright after being trampled. The blood seeped from wounds all down the body's left side, from just below the ear. The face, half of it, had a look of life. The bursts from one or more machine-guns had ripped up his side, down to his thigh. He had been wounded before arrival but had obviously been standing facing his killers, and had turned as the trigger was pulled, or as the first bullet made his body swivel.

Soon after our arrival, there came the police photographer and a police ambulance. The body was put on a stretcher and loaded into the ambulance. The sight of the body on its back, the head flopped over one end of the stretcher, with the face half shot out – one bloody eye and one good one staring up at the sky – made a good photograph. I kept the picture for some time in my terror file. But that image kept leaping out of the file and into my mind for weeks as I lay in bed awake at night.

I went to the cocktail-party and enjoyed it.

The next afternoon, I wrote the old man's and son-in-law's names at the end of the list which was the paper's attempt to keep account of those being killed on all sides. A few days later I had a dream in which a man with no face, smartly dressed, but with one side of his coat in tatters and bloody, entered the office, went to my desk and put my name at the end of the list.

I told friends about this dream, which was repeated on several nights, to clear myself of it. But it has never gone. I think it reflected a way of life which I am still trying to describe and the story of which I have rewritten many times, never satisfied that I have quite got it out of my system. My own callousness, cocktail-party first, returns with all the scenes.

I kept the list for many months. It became the only record of its kind up to the end of 1975, when I stopped. Members of militant groups came to take copies for their own reference or for publication; as the number of pages grew, the more trustworthy borrowed the original copy, the only one I kept. They copied it and returned it.

I was terrified one day when my list was included under some outrageous political commentary in a guerrilla-funded magazine. I knew it was my list because some of the transposed dates on my list were reproduced transposed. And later, at a friend's home, reading his accumulated political pamphlets and unaware of his political responsibilities, I found a circular which gave my name as the author of a valuable contribution to the cause. I had the circular and copies destroyed, but I shiver a little at the memory of that paragraph.

5

THE HANGOVER

February 1976

The portent of a *coup d'état* hung over Buenos Aires like a motorway traffic signal. There were innumerable rumours of conspiracy against the embarrassing government of President María Estela Perón, heir to the administration of her late husband; his selection of her as vice-president and successor was the last cheap jibe of a great comedian. The lull in political activity, traditionally associated with the first two months of the year, when Argentina suffers its worst heat wave, had been overlooked by the militants. The weather was mild, the heat of political violence was oppressive. The toll for 1975 had been 1,100 dead in political violence. The figures, kept at the *Buenos Aires Herald*, were conservative but the only ones available. For most newsrooms it was impossible to keep such figures because they felt they had to separate the good dead from the bad dead; and the contortions required to achieve such divisions discouraged compilation.

Sixty men, women and children had been killed in January.

The army, navy and air force had encouraged rumours about a *coup d'état* since the failure, just before Christmas, of an air force uprising. The failure had been due not to defeat, but to lack of support in the other services. Since then, the government was ridiculed in every headline, the bravado of the press an undignified retaliation for its toadying to a Peronism capable of instilling fear in the newsrooms until just a few weeks before. There was an unabashed crowing at every stumble of a preposterous administration. There was a tacit guarantee of freedom from punishment by the armed forces – whose monitors worked late into every night, their office lights burning for all to see – which checked the day's news, the coverage, the people and organs to be wary of, the targets for future reprisal. The armed forces had scented blood and they liked it.

Just before Christmas, the 'People's Revolutionary Army' had attacked the Domingo Viejobueno army arsenal southwest of Buenos Aires. The guerrillas had been heavily infiltrated by army intelligence. According to our count, 160 people had been killed that day, many of them teenagers, too young to think beyond the ideological claptrap of revolutionary sacrifice. Two score were murdered by the army commander when he had ordered his subordinates not to take prisoners. The army had lost seven: a captain, one lieutenant, a sergeant and four conscripts. Assorted victims had included a businessman and two truck drivers, killed in the crossfire; and a taxi driver who could not claim insurance to repair the roof of his car, marked with a strange ripple effect by a burst from a machine-gun – 'Act of war' was excluded from his policy. He finally collected by changing his claim to 'Act of God': damage by hail. The dead were buried in a mass grave at the Avellaneda cemetery. One mother had been given her daughter's hands, severed for fingerprinting, in a jar of formaldehyde.

We went on holiday, on our annual escape to Valeria del Mar, 220 miles south of the capital, to a quiet wide beach. My wife and I had escaped there each year since we had married, and as each of our children were born so they had been taken there.

Peace was assured by earth roads which, when it rained, became bogs. Electricity was supplied by one wire strung atop poles which looked no stronger than dried thistles against the sky. We always stayed in a flat in a large building facing the sea. The road south goes through Chascomús – where Scots had built a church with a neo-classical portico in the middle of the flat wilderness – through Dolores, Guido and Madariaga, frontier towns on the eastern edge of the Pampas. Their drabness was vaguely exciting because of the distant memory of native Indian raids, street fights and slaughter. There was beauty in the flatness of the land, in the shivering nights and sweating days which oppressed that highway.

The children heard the shot and we rushed out to see what it was about. Diego Muñíz Barreto told us that the shot had been fired by a man in a car, at a group of young men walking by. All had been in bathing trunks, walking in the late siesta heat. The attackers were from a right-wing group camping on the left side of the beach; the wounded youth and his mates had been identified as members of a left-wing organisation, camped on the right-hand side of the beach, most of them students. Within thirty-six hours most of the left-wing group had folded their tents and departed. The shot youth had been taken to the hospital in Madariaga, fifteen miles away. Before his parents had reached the hospital, provincial police had removed the wounded man to an unknown place. He disappeared.

Diego knew the gossip because he usually went down to the beach through the left-wing tents on the right side. He winced slightly as he passed on the description of the youth dropping, hit by the bullet. 'I've seen it before; people just drop or fall back in a small pile, like a shirt or a pair of trousers. There is no more convincing sign of death or serious damage than that drop. Death is not an athletic pirouette as in the cinema. Have you seen it?'

I admitted that I had not.

My memory of death was of a man falling forward, straight as a board, off a pavement; his forehead had hit the tram line on the cobbled street and it had sounded like an egg breaking. The man had stumbled out of a bar where leaders of rival factions in the dock workers' union had had an argument that had ended in shooting. The sound of bone and flesh on metal, vaguely like that of the tip of fingers smacking the back of a hand, multiplied several times, has made me flinch on hearing it each time since.

'You've been inside,' Diego said, and met a series of grimaces and gestures to indicate silence lest my children hear. He acknowledged with his eyebrows: 'But you are all right;

they didn't do anything to you?' I agreed. The concept of somebody being harmed under arrest was a very loose one: death, madness or maiming caused alarm; but detention with violence, even with a serious hiding, was demoted to insignificance, just a beating. It was a mechanism of self-defence in the observer, to avoid demonstrating too much alarm about what was superable. It was not indifference; there was still concern and sympathy, but the attitude to injury had changed.

Diego and I had last met over a year before, when he had been funding a political magazine and I had been asked to help him produce it. His office had been raided, the elegant white leather upholstery torn to shreds, the furniture splintered and his huge fishtanks smashed.

We liked one another and helped one another, and held a healthy distrust for one another. He had once threatened to kill me and I constantly mocked his politics, and those of his friends.

Diego was a *chanta*, what Argentines call a line-shooter, a person whose status is insufficient in his own eyes. He had the mouth of Harry Flashman, but all the reckless courage that George Macdonald Fraser's fictional bully lacked. Diego had been born into money, blessed with a patrician name, and educated at St George's College, founded in 1898 by the British community as a replica of an English public school.

He had sold his inherited property so as not to be labelled as a landowner, invested the proceeds in commercial activities and built a successful fishing company on the south Atlantic coast. As a member of parliament for the Peronist Youth, he had been criticised in corridors for his flamboyant, but less than youthful, appearance.

A reflection of his many worlds is to be found somewhere in *Time* magazine for 1973. For *Time* he spun a yarn of political dilettantism, with the help of a fellow parliamentarian and a friend, both business associates; he described them as his bodyguards, showed off guns, boasted on behalf of guerrillas, threatened nationalisations, drank wine from milk jugs at breakfast. And though the reporter fell for an outrageous tale,

his published story read, by accident, as one of deep understanding of the confusing local politics.

Diego was much in demand – more for his money than for
his political clout; in politics any form of influence becomes
valid.

We arranged to meet that evening, in his flat, for coffee.

He had not yet had supper when I arrived. He was cooking.
A sputter and hiss from a skillet on the two-ring gas stove har-
monised with the ocean and gave the breeze a powerful whiff
of the cooking sauce. The sound of the sea came in through the
window like a shout over the dunes every time a wave broke in
the shallow.

As darkness set in at the end of the short twilight, the breeze
dropped. Diego was cooking a delicious sauce, a *tuco*, with
the slowness and deliberation of an engineering project. It was
for the pasta he was going to give his children for supper. He
cut onions carefully, then garlic, added herbs, stood back,
studied the small hill on the chopping board, added more of
each and poured everything into the pan, where one kilo of
tomatoes cut small was bubbling lethargically.

Diego poured mussels into a pot of boiling water by the gas
ring and watched the shells open as the molluscs were scalded,
blowing a small burst of bubbles as they died. Diego whistled
softly, 'What a *tuco!*' His two daughters announced that
another guest was going to be late. 'Until he comes, we can
have a few drinks and talk,' Diego said.

With that introduction began one of the longest drinking
nights ever. Our moods moved from mirth to malice, to con-
descension and sympathy, to regret and recrimination. It was
a review of the last three years in politics in Argentina; there
could be no other subject in the country. While we drank, we
recalled the country's drunken orgy of the last thirty-five
months. We were in the time of the hangover, there was nothing left but lamentations.

Diego had been elected to parliament in the March 1973 elections, when barricade fixtures decorated fashion windows.
The establishment behaved as if the country, with almost 200

years of independence after 300 years as a Spanish colony, was an omelette that could be turned over to show a better side upwards, with the burned bits underneath; after all, the tasty part was inside.

In the interest of political science we were visited by students from every university in the Western world, who attended public gatherings with an air of achievement. We got Fulbright Scholars, Wilson fellows, St Antony's readers, California Marxists, and English snobs in bush jackets, encouraged by our local post-graduates, who thought there were at least a couple of articles for the quarterlies to be found in this.

Juan Perón, nearly senile, without his Evita who had made him the political hero he had become, but with a third wife, returned in June to a welcoming crowd of over one million, the largest ever in South America. There was shooting between rival groups of his followers. That was the day when everybody one had ever known seemed to have gone to the Ezeiza airport; old schoolfriends met there, carrying a pistol in each pocket, their own memory of their real name confused by the use of so many aliases. That was the day when some people went to watch, some to commit murder; a few men went to commit adultery; provincial aunts arrived on the free train service – special for that day – to look for lost nieces; and hundreds of thousands of citizens of all ages went in the belief that this was the day when all their problems would be solved.

Perón gave tacit approval to the coup in Chile, of which he was notified by a committee of several officers. That event put an end to the socialism and life of Salvador Allende, a well-intentioned man but finally ineffective.

One month later, Perón became Argentina's president in a rigged election. It was not the voting that was at fault, but the preparations made by his own party, seizing radio and television time to the detriment of all others. I voted for him, and cannot regret it even now, in the callous idea that politics would finish him: he was too old, and something better had to come later. How mistaken can political appraisal be?

He died nine months later on the first day of July, pursuing his politics even in death: it split the year neatly in the middle, so that he could not be thought committed to one half or the other.

His widow took lunch of cold cuts – an unfortunate choice – in a small office next to the Senate chamber where her husband lay in state for four days, while the queues of mourners stretched for a couple of miles, winding about the city blocks. Kissing the corpse was forbidden because it had begun to decompose. The great man himself had ordered no preservation treatment after death, probably in fear of the bruising that his second wife, Evita, had received, after his enemies had taxied the coffin about Europe to remove it from political passions in Argentina.

His widow took over as president and the press, in an immense aberration, found parallels between her and Queen Victoria and other leaders. She was assisted by her secretary, a man ridden with a fear of dying, an impotent diabetic, devoted to parapsychology. He was also the Social Welfare Minister. He had many good men murdered and he held the country, including the president, in his hand. In yet another ghoulish ceremony, Eva Perón's coffin was brought back from the attic in Madrid where Perón had kept it. The government announced that this was in the national interest.

For nineteen months, from the time of Perón's death to the time Diego and I sat down in Valeria del Mar to wait for the *tuco* to cook, for his other guest to arrive, and with drinks in our hands, the cruelty and the corruption we had seen had confounded the hardest of men. Yet we discussed it as an ordinary part of political life.

We were on our third drink, when Diego decided to open three bottles of wine in preparation for supper. He wandered about the flat in his swimming trunks and a ragged shirt that was buttoned at the top and opened over his paunch. He was barefoot, his toes smacking on the floor.

How many friends had we lost in nineteen months? It must have been dozens. He snatched a copy of *Jaws* in Spanish from

71

his son and opened the cover. There was an inscription in memory of one who had once owned the copy.

'We took it from his mother's house, to have a souvenir of the boy. We had to tell her he was dead.'

The boy, for he had been only twenty, had belonged to the ERP. He had been arrested and broken under torture. When released from arrest, his organisation had put him on trial for betraying secrets. But the guerrillas had freed him with a pardon, when they found that he had gone mad. Then the Montoneros had grabbed him for another revolutionary trial and, though requested not to press him too hard, had sentenced him to die by firing squad.

Diego berated the Montoneros, whose ally and occasional financial supporter he had been some years before, and regretted the lack of leaders in revolutionary politics. He recalled a few. John William Cooke, Juan Perón's lieutenant and ideologue, had died of cancer short of fifty, in 1968. Joe Baxter, the cunning revolutionary who had risen from a sordid anti-semitic nationalist terror group to fight in the guerrilla armies of Cuba and Vietnam; had been buried in the British Cemetery in Buenos Aires in 1973, after being killed in an air crash in Paris. José Luis Nell, whom Diego called a 'great' guerrilla, had his spine snapped by a bullet during factional disputes. In September 1974 he had been taken in his wheel chair to a dark road by the river Plate. A pistol had been put on his lap. He had put the barrel in his mouth and squeezed the trigger.

'All fucking good Irishmen,' Diego remarked.

During Mrs Perón's government, her secretary made kidnapping fashionable. It had previously been a reprehensible part of guerrilla fund-raising – which by the end of 1973 had totalled 170 people abducted and released, in exchange for ransom of 43 million US dollars. The police found kidnapping to be an effective form of retaliation. The secretary set an example, using his own ministry as headquarters for a private army into which retired and active police officers were recruited. Trade union leaders organised private armies; businessmen hired bodyguards who protected their own employers, but did not hesitate to abduct others. Members of the provincial police forces found that they had all the equipment and none of the complications, and joined the hunt for suitable kidnap victims. Senior army officers formed kidnapping syndicates or organised their protection. Colonels bought new flats and weekend houses, to be used alternatively for pleasure or as safe houses. Army officers abducted a stud owner, not for cash but for the transfer of ownership of a horse, and thereby knew the rare privilege of gaining access to the Tattersall Ring, administered by the Jockey Club.

Lloyd's of London's agents in Buenos Aires kept raising the premium on kidnapping insurance; customers flocked to their offices.

The fashion went all the way down the social line. In Munro, a working-class suburb, a woman with a babe in arms had the child snatched from her as she entered a grocery. Until she emptied her purse of her scant shopping money onto the pavement, the infant was not returned.

Buenos Aires became a city roamed by unmarked cars, usually Ford Falcons, supplied on a fleet order to police, but preferred by all for reliability at high speed and relatively low running cost. The cars were parked outside Government House, without a licence number to mar the bumper. They sped through the city ignoring lights; they were feared by the public, and the only man to campaign against their presence was the editor of the *Buenos Aires Herald*.

Inside these cars sat men in dark glasses and half open shirts, holding machine guns, wearing half a dozen chains around their necks, with Saint Christophers, crucifixes and Virgin Marys. They would sometimes travel home on the same train as I, or on the bus to the islands, late at night; they would turn up in bars by the *Herald;* or in restaurants on the *Bajo*. Buenos Aires is a city of nine million, but, like every big centre, for some it is a village. They read the advertisements for handcuffs in the evening papers; talked in half sentences; were paid a freelance fee by the builders of security vans to test the tempered windshields. If there was a hint of recognition, their reaction was always the same; a glance over their dark glasses, a wink and a shake of the head was an order that greetings were not possible because recognition did not exist, and neither did casual acquaintance.

Who were these men? How did they wake up? With whom? Did they love? How? There did not have to be anything logical about them; there was no need to explain them; but it would be interesting just to know the full story of twenty-four hours of their lives.

The last quarter of the third bottle of wine was emptied into the *tuco* pan. Diego decided to put the *tallarines* on to cook and give his children supper.

The kidnapped were seen both as prisoners and as hostages to be held to ransom. Abductions crossed political lines, in vengeance or reprisal. Gangs allied with the armed forces to attack the suspected sympathisers or known ideologues of the guerrillas.

In a matter of a couple of hours, women lost their men and children; middle-aged couples lost their three sons; a child was left alone; a man aged overnight, his eyes bulged, his cheeks sagged, his hair went dusty grey and brittle, as those he had cared and worked for all his life were torn from his home in the small hours of an ordinary day. Men in masks or without them, shouting or wordless, brutal or polite, destructive or charming, stormed a home and carried away a sought victim, and perhaps one or two others as well, because they were there.

Whole lifetimes became smothered dreams, destroyed in minutes by murderous nightmares and evil characters out of the most horrifying fantastic literature.

As the number of victims grew, the raiders became more violent. They were heavily armed men, sometimes high on drugs, the lowest minds in the services recruited for depravity.

Their chiefs publicly accused guerrillas of choosing easy targets in the forces when non-combatant officers were murdered. But in the reprisal attacks they did the same, picking off whole families, defenceless, because of their undisguised, honest, even if misguided, political sympathies.

Sometimes we would hear the story from officers still high on drugs, who would stop in a bar for coffee. Or they were just drunk, trying to fade the memory of action. Their assignments of cruelty had strange codes. They blocked their ears with rubber swimmers' plugs, and put the two-way radio at full volume, so that they did not have to hear the pleading of victims in the back seat, a man begging for mercy for a son; a son asking for his brothers' release, taking responsibility for uncommitted crimes in final acts of courage, last thrusts of preservation by the conscious mind. More often they were clubbed into unconsciousness and their heads rested on rags so that their blood would not soil the car seat. Then they were thrown by the roadside, their bodies shaken by dozens of bullets from several guns; then their bodies were destroyed by hand grenades.

Women who were to be killed were beaten, pushed, pulled, kicked, but seldom sexually abused. Those, who were to be detained and only later 'disappeared' or put to death, were raped, often before they were taken from their flats; and then again under torture and in their cells. Frequently. One man boasted that he liked to open his trousers and make women kneel and put his penis in their mouth as they cried. He said he liked the feeling of their warm tears and saliva. He had read about it in a magazine published in Holland.

A lieutenant who could not keep apace left the service. To keep him quiet, he was helped into a partnership with a ships' chandler. There he could smuggle North American cigarettes without difficulty or hindrance, while his chiefs remained in command.

Diego placed a very large bowl of *pasta sciutta* on the table just as his friend arrived. We celebrated his entrance, because of the timing and because he placed three bottles on the table, *Bodega Lopez 1971*; it was gentle, with the smoothness of those wines that age well.

Diego rushed through the introductions, ordered the man to sit down, and explained that we had talked of sad things and the wine was needed to cheer us. Some day, it would be my responsibility, Diego ordered, to write these things down. I laughed; nobody wrote these things; it was too dangerous.

We attacked the *tallarines* and the warmed bread with an appetite that ill became us.

'And did you hear about the Chileans' corpse dumping?' Diego asked.

Of course we had. That story had been broken by the *New York Times* in mid-1975 and reproduced locally by *La Opinión*. The Chilean government was accused of liaising with elements close to the Argentine government to dump Chilean detainees, who had died under torture, on Argentine soil and there be made to appear as killed in gun battles.

The news caused panic in the exile community in Buenos Aires, among the Chileans, Bolivians and Uruguayans, at one time sure that Argentina's constitutional administration offered them safety from the military pursuers in their own countries. The United Nations High Commission for Refugees was pressed by frightened exiles to find passports and new countries of refuge; the Uruguayan secret service increased its terror in Buenos Aires – as asylees were exposed in the panic – abducting refugees and sending them back to Montevideo in shackles.

One Bolivian journalist received a telephoned threat one day and a clear order to get out of Argentina. He told the anonymous caller that he had no passport and could not get one at the consulate in Buenos Aires. The line went dead.

He left his wife, who grumbled about his constant philandering. Within forty-eight hours he had struck a fairly meaningful relationship with a young North American girl, barely out of adolescence, eager to meet journalists as she had only just arrived on an Inter-American Press Association Scholarship. The affair ended after breakfast the next day. It was only a week later that she wrote to her bank in Coral Gables to report that she had lost her cheque-book.

After he had left the girl, it took him all that day to find a rubber-stamp shop in the banking district which would, for a substantial sum, add his name to hers on the cheque. He arranged an appointment with Captain C and another military officer at the Bolivian Consulate. He went to his flat and fetched his expired Bolivian passport and went to the appointment with the diplomats. He showed them the cheque-book; but they asked for cash in exchange for two visas. He agreed to have the cash in two days; they asked for three days, as they had to have time to steal rubber stamps and work on signatures and entries.

Only one exchange shop on the *avenida* would accept his cheques, and then only for up to 200 dollars. It was not enough. With the little money he had and using his Argentine identity card, he took the night boat to Montevideo. At least there he was safe from the threats and would have time to think.

He spent the next two days going from one newsroom to another asking for a job, to no avail. He borrowed a typewriter and wrote a totally fictitious news story of a bank raid and car chase through Montevideo and posted it to a newspaper in Quito. Some day, if he went to Quito, they would have the money for him.

On an impulse, he went to the telephone exchange, called his wife long distance, apologised to her, swore love everlasting and asked if she would do him a favour.

He asked her to do the following:

Would she telephone Captain C at the Bolivian Consulate in Buenos Aires and tell the officer that her husband had to go to Montevideo because of a death threat. She should say that her husband had not run out on the Captain and had promised that if the Captain took the night boat to Montevideo, her husband would refund the fare and pay the agreed price for the two visas. Her husband regretted that he did not have cash, but would give the Captain a certified cheque for the full sum.

Then the journalist went to the Bank of the Republic branch at the port end of Plaza Independencia in Montevideo and to the shipping department. He found the clerk and asked for the documents of a ship he knew was in Galveston or thereabouts. As the clerk turned, the Bolivian glanced at the rubber stamps on the counter. One said 'Bank of the Republic – Bill of Lading Inspected'. It would have to do. He quickly used it on a blank cheque. When the clerk returned with the expected reply he left the bank. He spent the last of his cash on another day in Montevideo and on one telephone call in which he was assured that Captain C would be on the night boat.

The transaction was simple and friendly. The passports were duly stamped. The Bolivian and his wife went to live in Mexico City.

Diego got hiccups and the other man nearly choked as we all laughed at the story for twenty minutes.

Diego said we ought to go for a walk and drink some coffee on the beach. It was nearly half past three; I was shivering as the warming effect of the alcohol left my body and only the damaging effect on my sense of balance remained. We did not go to the beach but to a *boite* on the corner where Diego persisted in pointing to several young men he said had shot the youth the day before. We bought three rounds of cognac and admired the women.

At five o'clock we went for a walk. The sky over the sea was beginning to change from black to grey; a suggestion that we drink for another hour to wait for sunrise was accepted.

I left to the sound of Diego's voice complaining that 'We have not discussed any of the things I wanted to see you about!'

I stumbled into the flat and left a trail of clothes between the door and the bed. I slept late and the hangover, when I tried to get up, was overwhelming. After that we saw Diego twice, on the beach, and when we returned to Buenos Aires I saw him no more.

Diego was murdered, after arrest by police, in February 1977.

6

ASSIGNATION HOTEL

April 1976

The woman mispronounced my surname. When told that she had whom she wanted, there was a pause; then something that sounded like 'Hmm...' There followed another pause. The line crackled, then came a halting introduction. 'My name is María Eugenia... You do not know me... Though perhaps you might remember me...'

I sighed and waited. It was the typical preface to a plea for assistance; the search for a common acquaintance, so that the listener did not lose interest and with an apology cut off.

'I went with you to a political meeting about a year ago because you did not know where it was... Remember? We met in a bar and then took the train together...'

The picture of a fair-haired woman, young, early twenties, began to take shape.

'I would like to see you,' she said.

She could not come to the newsroom, but wanted the meeting to take place that night. I could not leave the paper before half past one.

'I don't even know if I am going to see you. I don't know you, don't know who you are with or where you are and how long it will take me to go to see you...'

'I am alone,' she said. 'I am at an assignation hotel.'

An assignation hotel was a dangerous meeting place. For the past two years guerrillas, as well as other political groups, had used assignation hotels as points of reunion. The discretion offered by the management was conducive to unhindered progress in political discussion. But in morality-conscious

Buenos Aires, which had closed brothels years ago and had ordered brighter lighting in the nightclubs so that even the bar girls wore bras, police raided the assignation hotels occasionally. They checked the proprietors' licences and the guests' documents, forcing coitus interruptus as an institutional hazard. In one raid, four couples had been found, fully-clothed, chatting in one room. The explanations that they had been planning an eightsome were dismissed on the grounds that the manager had no licence for more than two people to a room. At the police precinct they were identified as political activists. The discovery led to an intensification of the frequency of raids on assignation hotels.

I told the woman that the meeting place was inappropriate; there was a whimper in her voice when she said that she could arrange no other.

We agreed that she would call again at twenty past one, to say if it was all right to meet.

There were no buses on the street. It was a new feature of Buenos Aires. Until the military coup, a month before, buses had run till long after midnight. There was nobody on the streets now to justify a bus service. People scurried home from work, so as not to get involved in what they feared most: political incidents. I walked along the centre-island of the wide Leandro Alem Avenue to Retiro, then along Libertador Avenue for two hundred yards and turned off, walking uphill to an old squat building, its front windows shuttered at pavement level. This was the Hotel of Flowers. It was behind the Palace of Flowers, the Buenos Aires flower market which became a dance hall on Saturday and Sunday nights, frequented by maids seeking entertainment, and middle-class teenage males in search of their 'debut'—their first sexual experience. The boys' parents accepted this, even with their own maids—as long as it was not in the servants' room. The boys' mothers pretended not to know and their fathers looked serious, solemnity disguising their mischievous pride.

The entrance passage was tiled in green with relief flowers on the walls and with crosses and diamonds laid out into a pattern on the floor. It looked dark, smelt damp; nowhere was there a flower to adorn the round-the-clock act of love in this Hotel of Flowers.

I stood in a tiled patio, roofed with green corrugated plastic sheet; on the four walls shuttered doors stared darkly at the open space. A man looked up from a reception desk on which a small lamp lit the pages of the late evening edition, his reading exhausted except for the small ads.

The man pointed the way down the passage to Room 23, and snapped at my departing back: 'May you enjoy your stay.'

I stopped, protesting: 'Look here, I am a married man; I have children... I don't need this squalid...' The porter's hands, at right angles to his arms, were open, patting the air in a gesture of calm as his puckered lips emitted a hissing sound. When silence had been restored, the porter's left hand dropped to his side and the right hand turned, palm up, pointing along the passage; the corners of his mouth stretched back across his cheeks in the thinnest of smiles, like a clock at a quarter to three.

My watch said it was nearly two.

I peered at the door numbers as I walked down the passage. I thought whispers could be heard from behind the doors, but it must have been my imagination.

My thoughts concentrated on the woman I was going to see. Memory shaped a face, though I knew little about her. She had been my guide over one year before, when I had attended a semi-clandestine press conference. The guide, who had now called herself María Eugenia on the telephone, had met me in the bar of a hotel on Avenida de Mayo. She was an attractive young woman, dressed in a black velvet trouser suit. Her short fair hair had framed a long face with high cheek bones. Her carriage and her elegance had given her that beauty which seemed to be the privilege of some Argentine women alone among their sisters in the rest of the world. I had been delighted with the improvement in political public relations. We had taken a train into the suburbs but had arrived too early to be admitted to the dance hall rented by the Montoneros guerrillas for their first party congress: over a hundred people from all over the country who had been gathered for the occasion under the very noses of the police. The attractive guide had decided that we should go for a walk in the time we had. She had questioned me at length about my acquaintance with her chief, Montoneros leader Mario Eduardo Firmenich, whom I had met before. She had never met the chief, being only a minor member of the organisation and her husband only a delegate to the congress.

I had not been prepared to talk indefinitely about her commander, so matters had become personal. She was pregnant and took the conversation to that subject. I had teased her that she had conceived the night before, her thin curvaceous figure betraying nothing; with a twinkle in her happy eyes, she had grinned. We drank several cups of coffee at a bar, discussing the benefits of natural childbirth with a supportive mate and a co-operative doctor. I asked her if she had a house, where she would live and what her plans were for the future child. She had seemed to have little to do with politics, and the only time she had mentioned them had been to say that she hoped the bad times would soon be over, though her expression had no conviction. As we had walked back from the bar to the hall, she had held my hand. Later I wanted to think that it had been an act of friendship, a sign of intimacy after the conversation; but probably it had been a tip that she had been given on how to present an appearance of lovers to dispel suspicion. I had held dear the memory of that afternoon with her and hoped that she, and her child, had survived the bloody months that had followed.

I tapped softly on the door and heard the spring of a bed. The door opened a crack and a head moved into the slit of light. She opened it wider and flopped back onto the bed as I entered. I leaned against the closed door and looked at her, then around the room. It had the tall ceiling of the old fashioned houses and was a section of a larger room which had been partitioned. Along one deep green wall was a coat rail with hangers, on one of which were her overcoat and scarf. Her handbag stood on a brown metal night table by the bed. On the wall over the headboard was a small wooden cross with a plastic Christ. The wall opposite the bed had a tyre company calendar and a print with a lake and hills, framed in plastic imitation wood. In the fourth wall, opposite the coat rail, there was a door to a shower, basin, lavatory and bidet. There was a large mirror over a long table which had replaced a dresser, and next to it a covered sewing machine.

I nodded my head, lips pursed, hands behind my back against the door in a studied pose of disapproval.

'They use this as the ironing room—that's why they've got the table and the sewing machine,' she explained.

I looked at her again. She was not the sweet young girl I had felt paternally lecherous about one year before. She looked thin, but without the cultivated svelteness that she had displayed at the last meeting. It was a drained body; her eyes, small and without sparkle, looked out from dark pits; her once short shiny hair was long, which might also have been attractive; but it was unwashed, dull and matted.

I smiled at her: 'Last time I saw you we talked about your pregnancy, remember? What happened to your child?'

She returned the smile, a tiny grimace which reflected pain inside. Her hand moved in front of her face to wave the subject away.

'A boy,' she said. 'Stillborn; in September 1974. It was after we had been ordered to go underground.'

It had been too much for this small fragile person. The Montoneros, having lost several members to the guns of rival Peronist factions and of the police, had ordered all their branches to go into hiding. It was meant to be an act of defiance against the government of General Perón's widow, María Estela Perón. It was much publicised, but costly. Underground action is not only dangerous, but also a strain on any constitution. Those who had been underground before could endure the new transfer; surface activists, with no preparation for living clandestinely, suffered most. They were picked off like flies by their enemies.

'What is it you need? Where is your husband?' I expected her to say that she was divorced.

'Dead.' She looked up, 'Didn't you know? Oh, of course

not...' The thin hand waved backwards in front of her face dismissing my ignorance as understandable because of censorship. 'He was killed last week, in that ambush on the flat in Chacarita.' She shrugged, I thought, with irony, because the death had occurred in an area of Buenos Aires best known for its cemetery.

'When? I mean, what day was it? Was he alone?' My questions were urgent, anxious for the information, to have the details for the record. It seemed so important to keep a record of these actions, of the deaths. I remembered a police statement at the end of the previous week which said that four 'seditious elements, members of a terrorist gang', had been killed in a gunbattle when they had resisted arrest. There had been no casualties among the security forces. I realised that in my concern for a death tally I had ignored her feelings.

'Sorry,' I said. 'How did it happen?'

Ruben, her husband, and three others had been living in the flat for a few days, a 'safe' house where the Montoneros guerrillas had sent some of their less competent or more exposed members. It turned out to be unsafe. There had been no gunbattle, but a summary execution.

'*Montos* [Montoneros] miscalculated,' she said. 'They never thought it would be like this. They thought they could stay hidden and weather the worst; but the army came in with a list of the people they wanted, everywhere; they knew everything. They tortured those they could squeeze for something, then killed them. *Montos* never thought it would be so fast. It'll take time to reassemble.'

This was the only way to get information. Four weeks after the March coup the military government had become annoyed with the few papers which persisted in reporting the appearance of bodies in ditches, parks or cars, and had ordered that no deaths, abductions or arrests could be reported or victims identified without official permission. I had to remember the date of the death of Ruben and his three mates for what was referred to in the newsroom as the 'scorecard'.

'What do you want me to do?' I asked, finally moving away from the door to sit by her on the bed. She did not look up, but stared at the floor.

'I want to get out and I need help.'

'Why did you call me?'

'I was told you could help. Several people had your name,' she said. It filled me with a sense of importance, which seemed hardly responsible; but there must have been some part of the subconscious that determined the feelings a man used for survival – and vanity may have been one of them.

'I need money and an identity document to get me to Brazil. Mine's no use; it has my married name on it,' she said.

'What about your parents?'

'I can't call them. The telephone could be tapped or the house watched. If they come to me I would be caught. Anyway, I haven't seen them for over a year; they probably don't want me now of all times. They hated Ruben; he wasn't Jewish. No, I've got to go, far away; I've got an aunt in New York and another in Israel. I've got to keep running till I reach one of them and only then call my parents.'

I asked her for her mother's telephone number just in case and scribbled it on my train ticket. 'How about all the lawyers and faddish followers; can't they help?'

'I don't know where to find them. All right, you can't or don't want to help. I understand. Sorry I made you come.' Then she panicked at the sound of her own words and looked up with frightened eyes. 'Please help.'

'I was hoping there might be somebody more practical. I'll do what I can.'

'There are no lawyers, no groups of support; nothing. The army had a list of them all in November. I know a retired general who memorised part of the list and recited it to a lawyer friend, with the advice to get out...'

'And...'

'He went to Venezuela in December.'

'If you knew that why didn't you get out too?' I asked with genuine curiosity.

'Because you can never believe that the "death lists" are true; because you are convinced that things must blow over,

85

simply because it is such a nuisance to move, because Ruben was hooked on gaining rank in the organisation; and because they had us hooked, we couldn't get out... I suppose you will say that we should not have gone underground in 1974...'

'You never did, *mi amor*. You never could. It's not your fault...' I was feeling sleepy from a long day and night's work and its tension. I stood to take the drone out of my voice. 'Politics of action are not for the middle class. They are for the very rich or for the very poor. The one keep account of themselves and record their failures as victories with critical biographies and funeral monuments. The other die and are forgotten. Those in the middle are too concerned with their future prospects to do anything right in the present. You should have been breeding or making a career; your Ruben should have been working hard to pay for the flat, the car and the weekend plot in the future. That is what middle-class activism is for.'

My voice was monotonous in spite of standing up and I watched my lips in the mirror. 'I was at the press conference when your great chief advised: "To those who want to stay in the middle, we suggest that they step aside when the war starts." If any one can hate a man for his words, it would be your chief for that sentence. So smart, so murderous: with that one sentence he made hundreds of people think they had to decide on a side; they tried to hide, and thereby had decided ... to die.' At any other time, I would not have been angry over such a matter; but at that moment it seemed something suitable to attack. Anger was momentarily fortifying.

'What did you do?' she asked. Her voice surprised me; it was cold and sharp and a reminder that she was there.

Without turning I said: 'Stayed in the middle. As always.'

'Yes, you're in the middle, but not neutral: you're right in the middle of the mess.'

That woke me. She was too cutting and too true. I swung round as she stood. In her right hand she held a police regulation Colt .45; it was cocked.

I held a shivering hand in front of me, fingers wide open.

86

'That's cocked,' I informed her. 'You'll have everybody in here if you shoot. Please be careful.' Her finger was near the trigger.

'You've got to help me,' she said through clenched teeth. But then her eyes filled with tears, and the gun hand fell by her side like a wet rag. I held my breath and moved away; but the gun remained there, at the end of her fingers. She looked up and I stared at her tearful eyes. She put the gun down and came towards me. 'Sorry,' she sobbed. I put my arms around her drooping shoulders. She started to cry, slowly at first, then more audibly until finally her body shook with sobs.

After a few seconds, I told her to uncock the gun. She turned away and went to the bed, picked up the gun, held the hammer, pumped the barrel back and then slid it into position, catching an unfired bullet as she did so. She removed the magazine from the butt, popped the bullet back in with the other five and snapped the magazine home, then put the gun on the night table. And stood looking at me.

I stepped past her, opened the bed, sat her down, lifted her feet, taking off her shoes as I did so, and put her legs on the bed. As I covered her with the blanket, the stains on her tartan skirt became more noticeable; the thin black polo-neck sweater was also speckled with dirt.

At the door I said, 'Good night. Try to sleep. I promise to come back in the morning with whatever I can get.'

In the street my legs felt very weak and I walked with careful steps along the sheltered pavement of the avenue towards the station. It had become urgent that the girl left the country. If she was caught, mine would be among the first names she would give; because I would have been one of the last persons she had seen, and because her training would determine that those outside her organisation should be the first to be sacrificed under interrogation.

There was one friend who had offered money and documents some months ago, foreseeing trouble. It seemed best to call him first thing in the morning.

María Eugenia's husband had been the more involved of the two, and she had decided to make a break. If she had resorted to the organization for help they might have hidden her for a time, but soon would have made her enter action as part of a cell. It was, according to some stories which had done the rounds of newsrooms, one ruse for recruitment by guerrillas: they offered a person protection and a place of hiding, then compromised their charge, and the person was irremediably committed, in the eyes of the guerrillas and the police. The future then could only be further involvement, greater commitment by whatever action was ordered.

The stories of recruitment may have been military propaganda; but they had a ring of truth to them which had made some journalists accept them, especially when applied to provincial cities, where communities were smaller, and political affiliations better known. According to one account, if a wayward militant or unarmed fringe sympathiser refused to join an underground cell, a gun was planted in his home, and then police were tipped about the existence of the gun in the house. Once the raid had taken place, the man became wanted. Protection was then offered by guerrillas. Another way was for guerrillas to enter a person's home, turn everything upside down and then leave. When the occupier returned and found evidence of a search, he panicked and sought cover from a cell. Reception was said to be sympathetic, but after a few days action was organised. The newcomer was ordered into the back of a car, which was used for an attack on police or on a bombing spree. From then on that person was involved.

Some of this seemed most unlikely. But in times of uncertainty, no rumour, no story was light enough to be dismissed; a person could never get far enough from rumours and events to analyse them with any clarity.

The tower clock in front of Retiro – a replica of Big Ben, and given in token gratitude to Argentina for being the cornerstone of the British economy for half a century – struck a quarter to three as I went into a station bar for a glass of wine and a piece of hot cheesy pizza. There was almost an hour to wait for the next train.

My chewing accelerated as I thought of María Eugenia, of the terrible torture methods newsrooms heard about those days, and of the recruiting methods of the guerrillas. I gulped the wine and ran back to the hotel. I wanted to have a last look at her, say a few comforting words before going home. My legs were carrying me at a fast pace when I crossed the empty avenue and ran back along the covered pavement. The night porter ignored me on my way down the passage.

She had taken off her clothes down to her petticoat. She got back into bed as I entered the room, which was warm and fuggy. I sat down on the bed.

'I had to come back to see how you were. I left in such a rush.'

I took off my raincoat and flung it on the table, then sat down again, still panting. 'You waved that gun at me and I just wanted to get out...'

'I've never fired a gun in my life...'

'I thought so. I wanted to make sure you were comfortable.' She smiled; a pale, cheerless, smile. 'Well, I'll make my way back.' I reached for the raincoat. Only two minutes had gone by since I had entered the door.

'Thank you for coming. You ran.' I nodded. 'Thank you. They told me you had courage...' I must have looked embarrassed. 'Really.' I wished she, or 'they', had not said that. It was not true. My return to the room had been prompted by the selfishness generated by uncertainty; by the desire to know that she was at peace; her own peace of mind was of less importance than was my own. Uncertainty about her safety would have preyed on the conscience. And my conscience was already overladen with worry about people who might have known me and who had 'disappeared' after raids by security personnel, or been taken into detention at unknown places of imprisonment. At times it became a relief to know that a missing person was dead, the search had come to an end, the suffering had stopped. Concern for the disappeared, the imprisoned, the persecuted and threatened was natural and necessary. The concern was selfish because it reflected a determination to survive by securing the survival of others. For survival was the only victory to be achieved. If feelings could be seen as a will to survive, then I had courage.

María Eugenia had courage, expressed in the selfishness of her plea for help and in her gratitude at my return.

My thoughts took me away from the room for a moment and I didn't notice her sit up in the bed and stare at me. Her arms were crossed in front of her, her hands on her shoulders. 'Hey, where are you?' she asked. I blinked and saw her, with a very pale face and lines of dirt on her neck. Her small breasts were ballooned by her arms which pressed them upwards and her nipples peeped through the lace border at the top of her petticoat.

Her cheek was ready for a parting kiss when I leant forward. She dropped back on the pillow, which had a large brown stain at one end, probably a drink spilled by another patron. She did not return my greeting, but turned her face to the wall which had the clothes rail.

'Stay a little more... And make love to me,' she said.

'I can't,' I snapped in the manner of an order. Yet although my heartbeat filled my ears to shut out whatever she said next and the beat filled the entire room, her request seemed a normal reaction given the surroundings. Finally, I could hear her voice again.

'Please... I want to; I need to ... to start again. Help me,' she whispered.

I lay down beside her without removing my clothes, not even my jacket and tie. My arm went under her head and almost immediately my nose started to itch. As my free hand came up to scratch the irritated point, she took the hand and put it on a breast. She turned from lying on her back to face me as I grimaced to remove the itch in my nose. With a small laugh her hand came up to rub my face, then she buried her face in my shoulder. In a distant voice, muffled by my coat, she said, 'I have not made love for ages, it was no longer a marriage with Ruben. We were on the run all the time, always with people around us, never a minute alone. Please make love to me!' Her voice was urgent.

But nowhere in my body was there even the smallest sign of a physical stirring. I was hampered by the disturbing thought of infidelity; and worse, of being inadequately unfaithful.

With my hand on her breast I was mentally removed to the recollection of Albert Camus' *A Happy Death* where the character, Mersault, wondered at the capacity of a woman to take into herself a large part of a total stranger. A body had to be known to be made intimate, its smell, its touch, its taste tested before parts could be bonded... My hand moved from her breast and slid under the sheet to her crotch; the fingers combed her pubic hair and moved further until the index found the soft damp folds. Her body moved again and she turned her face to the wall, looking towards the clothes rail. The fingers moved and turned gently. After a short while, her eyes still open, a whimper rose from her throat. Suddenly her back arched and she remained, trembling, raised from the sheet for what seemed a long time; the muscles in her thighs tightened and I pulled my hand away when she seemed to be about to crush my knuckles.

Then she relaxed. After an interminable silence, I took my arm from under her head and got off the bed. I felt awkward, clinical in the coldness; she had been the recipient of a technical service. I could feel her staring at my back.

'Are you annoyed because I...?'

'Not at all, I'm just going to wash my hands.'

She had fallen asleep by the time I had put on my raincoat. As I lifted the bed clothes to cover her better, a burst from a machine-gun filled the quiet night. Another burst followed, then the bang of four high-calibre bullets.

The sound came from not too far away and I felt afraid. The streets would be dangerous because of the firing; but more because the police would be out in great numbers and it was inconvenient to be stopped at this time of night. I wondered what had happened. It could have been a raid by police on political suspects. They would have been met by fire – death was better than detention under the new military government. It might also have been a police car ambushed by guerrillas; maybe a couple of uniformed men, killed for being the sentinels of tyrants by the armed hand of those wishing to be despots. Fear dissipated to be replaced by a vacuum, a deep depression caused by unattributable grief.

I snorted at my own faint-heartedness. Here I was tucking in a minor political activist's widow and regretting the suspected deaths in a gun-battle. The deaths should have made me angry, not melancholy. But anger was not one of my emotions – that was why I was in the middle. Even if it was a non-neutral middle: the middle of the mess, as María Eugenia had said.

Civil conflict grew out of political enmity; but far more out of personal emotions, which were invoked as motives for revenge. Individuals set out to avenge a militant blasted to bits by a grenade; an officer decided to avenge his colleague and became the target of another's vengeance. The casualties grew; the leaders of rival factions assumed responsibility for the outrages and then ordered an increase in terror as a way of keeping their authority, of trying to win control of the wayward in their faction. That was when conflict could become war.

The machine-guns burst again; the sound echoed in the night and I imagined the detonations rising into the air like a wisp of smoke in the clear autumn sky. After a long moment packed with gunfire, perhaps as much as one minute, the wail of police sirens replaced the bullets. This was the sound of Buenos Aires, the sound of strife; a type of music, the bullets providing the percussion, and the sirens a funeral organ in the city's very own death march.

María Eugenia did not stir. I put the light out and left the room. At the corner near the station, there were small clusters of the derelicts of the night looking along the avenue to where the sound of shots had come from. About a mile away, the avenue was cut off by patrol cars with flashing lights. I went to take the train.

With a fat wad of one hundred thousand pesos notes for her fare in one pocket, but with a sense of relief that I had not entered the complicated wrangle of trying to get her a forged identity document, I walked from the station to the hotel. With my head down against a chilly mid-morning wind, as if I were staring at my thoughts on the pavement, I walked into the hotel.

A huge hand leapt out of a black cuff and locked on the front of my shirt.

'How did you get in?' I was asked by a face above a dark suit.

'By the door,' I stammered.

The grip was released; the hand was trembling. It was the hotel manager; he had been warned by the nightwatchman to look out for the visitor of the night before. There had been two police at the door since last night. If they were not there now, it was because they had probably gone for a cup of coffee; but really they should not have left, because they had to wait for the investigating magistrate.

Early in the morning there had been a gunfight between guerrillas and police at another hotel just down the road. Several guerrillas had been killed and one policeman had been decapitated by a burst from a machine-gun. Police had searched every assignation hotel in the area. The nightwatchman had warned all the couples in the rooms to leave, but the girl in number twenty-three had stayed. When a police corporal had opened the door she shot him between the eyes and wounded two plainclothesmen; police had fired what might have been up to one hundred bullets into her body.

The hotel manager gripped my arm: 'I don't know what it was about; but I suspect it was political. I won't say anything. It's bad for business if we tell. Pay me for the room and get out. You don't want to risk getting yourself in the middle of this mess.'

7

THE SHAME AND
THE ANGER

May 1976

A mother came to the *Buenos Aires Herald* in the evening. She had tried to get help to find her daughter everywhere else. She had been to police stations, courts, hospitals; called influential friends and finally had gone to the newspapers. Each news editor in town had told her, quite unabashed, that he could do nothing and that she ought to try the English-language paper, the smallest in the city. It was known that the *ingleses* stuck their neck out. We were suspected of having the protection of the British and United States embassies, as if such missions were capable of protecting anything. Any argument appeared unaccountably solid when it was necessary to deflect responsibility in times of crisis. But she was told that the *Herald* was the only paper that would report the news of her daughter's disappearance. The publicity might help if she went back to the police stations, army depots, courts and rabbis that she had resorted to earlier in her hopeless pilgrimage.

She had been advised of her daughter's arrest by an anonymous caller using a public telephone not far from where the girl had been picked up. The caller had made sure he was speaking to the right person, apologised for not introducing himself, and described how and where the girl had been arrested.

The mother was short, plump, with hair slightly greying and with an almost unlined face. Her features were tender, as of fantasy mothers men and women conjure when their minds fly for refuge to a home long left.

Her hand was limp and dry as I took it with a politely muttered invitation that she come into the newsroom. She dropped into a chair with a tired sigh.

'I am the mother of a person who has disappeared; so please listen.' She apologised for coming. She was asking for only a little guidance, no help. 'I was told that this paper would publish something about what happened to her.' She paused and stared at me; I looked away. 'I don't want anything published now . . . I want you to help me find her.'

I told her I had been advised that she was coming, which was untrue; but it gave her the impression, even if a small one, that somebody else had cared about her as she had walked from another newspaper office, across the Plaza de Mayo and along the avenue south of Government House by the large mausoleum-like building of the army command and the turn-of-the-century anachronism that was the Custom House.

An office boy brought her a cup of tea and she hardly let it touch the desk top before she had raised it to her lips.

'I decided when I sat down that I had come for a chat with nice people and some comfort. Just the fact that you've invited me in makes you people better.' I glanced at my watch and wondered how long she would stay. Humanitarian consideration and newsroom deadlines were in conflict.

Her husband was under sedation since they had received the news. They had not seen their daughter for months and did not know what had happened to her husband, an engineer; she had been led into the 'political thing' by him. She sniffed at the hint of tears and opened her handbag; but instead of a handkerchief she produced a small crumpled paper with a list of all the names and addresses of places she had called at to try to find her daughter.

She sighed deeply at regular intervals, wondering aloud why there were people so cruel that they had decided that she should not know the whereabouts of the girl.

'When I was young, people were tortured, people were killed by police. But it was just one or two and people did not worry, because it was known that something strange was going on . . . they were involved in something . . . they were criminals, or anarchists. . . But now they are taking away people by the dozen, by the hundreds I think . . . I was told today, I suppose you know: there were over two hundred writs of habeas corpus filed in the central courts building last week ... over two hundred in one week, just at the central courts, which cover only a small part of the federal capital ... And the military authorities and police always answer the same: The person mentioned is not being held, there is no warrant for the arrest of the citizen in this jurisdiction ... etc.

'I don't have a photograph, but you should have seen her ... You would love her. Of course, you will say it is just her mother speaking, but she is beautiful, so tender, such a loving girl. And she was always such a friend to me.'

My mind wandered to Arthur Koestler's character who said that the faults of the Left were to be seen in the ugliness of its women; but such faulting did not apply to many young women in what for a time was the fashionable, non-dialectic vernacular Left. It seemed to draw women who were quite attractive.

She continued in praise of her daughter, overruling by persistence my efforts to interrupt her. Finally I forced my way into her monologue by remarking that something should be done to get some information. After almost two minutes of uncomfortable silence, we started to discuss the possibility of some kind of publication. 'Mrs —— reported yesterday that according to anonymous callers her daughter ...'

She could also pay for a personal announcement in the other newspapers. There was another pause for thought and a new idea, one which had not been tried by us yet. She should go to the Roman Catholic hierarchy, who might have contacts with the army. The Catholic Church intervening for a Jewess; we laughed for the first time. She took the name of a visiting Spanish Jesuit who might help, and few questions asked; it would be dangerous to compromise local Jesuits or the Irish Passionist Fathers, who were being slandered anonymously as favouring the Left; a dangerous, as well as untrue and unnecessary, accusation. She said thank you for the cup of tea and left.

She seemed tougher than many of the people who had come to the paper in ever-increasing numbers. I wondered if persistence in the pursuit of her daughter's whereabouts would ever be successful.

Immediately after the 24 March 1976 *coup d'état* there had been an unbroken stream of people coming to report the abduction of relatives by members of the security forces. There seemed no limit to the concept of vengeance against those who had been identified with the Left in the previous four years of political instability, whether they were militants or sympathisers. Wives – widows, really – said that their husbands, trapped in a flat, had been flung out of windows to death below. Others had been battered unconscious on the pavement in front of their homes, before they were taken away. Their children and wives, when all had not been carried away, had been woken to watch the torment of the man they loved, as the houses were systematically looted. At one home the raiders had arrived with a van in which to remove everything, from the contents of the bathroom medicine cabinet to the washing machine. Some children were taken with the parents and disappeared, some were left on the pavement, with a cardboard notice hung from a string round their necks, with their name and address scrawled on the board.

Some women burst into tears as they spoke of their men or their children; some parents made elegant introductions as if it were beneath them to appeal for help: their own politics having nothing to do with those of their children, trying to show an aloof concern for their issue. One man arrived at midday in the newsroom with a copy of a writ of habeas corpus and asked that it be reported, but that his address be omitted. Three hours later he returned, asking that no publication be made: 'I have done all I can for my son; he was old enough to know in what he had got himself involved.' There was no convincing him that the younger man might not have been involved. He left in tears but wanted no publication; he had a job to keep and wanted no problems.

The editor fumed, ranted. How could people disown their children? How could they forget them like they might an umbrella in the train or lose them like a dog in the street? But he fumed alone. In fact, most editors held him in contempt for risking his paper in the cause of individual rights and civilised morals; the armed forces were merely using tough methods to rid the country of the threat from the Left. Remember Algeria? they asked. Well, these were Algerian methods.

The commander of the first army corps in Buenos Aires showed immense charity towards the men and women who arrived at the Palermo barracks each morning to plead for help to find their spouses or their children; the night before he had organised and directed the raids that had caused those people to disappear. The Córdoba army corps commander, who had authority over most of central Argentina, laughed in the faces of parents who pleaded for information. The navy, at its mechanics school on the Buenos Aires northern riverside and next to the River Plate soccer stadium, experimented with the most terrible torture methods in testing the resistance of captives, and were rumoured to be using bandsaws to amputate the limbs of their victims.

Each day we debated how to report each new account of human outrage; in every edition we dared only to give a fraction of what we were told. Egocentrics like myself, with knightly fantasies, imagined scenes akin to killing monsters and saving beautiful women. But fantasies, anger, anguish and probing did not produce sufficient column space for denunciation. Frustration led to an increased intake, alone or in company, of *demi-tasses* of black coffee and glasses of *cognac* at the corner bar, *El Nido* (the Nest), where credit made custom more regular.

The paper decided to check with the police headquarters in the Buenos Aires province capital, La Plata, 30 miles south of the city of Buenos Aires – the country's federal capital – because it covered a wide area in which several dozen people had 'disappeared'. I had been to school in La Plata, to a technical college where I had spent a year pursuing what I suspected would be a great future as an engineer. I could not remember learning anything, or passing a single examination, but had thoroughly enjoyed that year there. I had played truant day after day to spend hours each afternoon in La

Plata's Natural History Museum or, with fellow truants, testing a home-made .22 short-barrel pistol against sparrows in the zoo, or just rowing on the lake by the museum.

That was the La Plata I had enjoyed, a provincial capital whose detractors classified its population into three occupations – lawyers, students and prostitutes. In the last three years political factionalism had turned the city into a battleground. It had something sinister about it now, even if that was only my imaginary addition to its wide cobblestone streets.

At the tall police headquarters building there were sentry boxes on each corner, and concrete parapets concealed the ground floor windows; entry up the enormously wide steps was reduced to a passage marked by two sets of crowd control railings. I had to state that I wanted information for an article in tribute to police slain in combat with guerrillas to get past the main door security-check to the press office. I was frisked there, and on entry and exit from the lifts. My beard made me suspicious and they were reticent with every answer. Even the smart young officer who handled public relations was curt. When the door finally closed behind me in the office of the commissioner on duty, I asked for details of deaths, of police and others. I also enquired about political detainees.

He produced a neatly typed list of his force's casualties, dead and wounded – name, age and number of dependants; then flung a wad of daily police reports on the desk and told me I had ten minutes to look through them. There were very few names, one or two I recognised; but the few who were identified were mostly common criminals. The rest were dead and had 'NN', no name, in the space for identification.

I was questioned as to my motives, admonished for my interest in dead subversives. 'You don't want to write about them. Who wants to know about them? They are dirt, best forgotten.'

In the next few days we travelled to as many cities with regional police commands as possible. Quilmes, Pilar, Campana, Chascomús, Madariaga, Mar del Plata... Some were suburbs, others resorts visited recently, others were only memories of youth, where I had been taken by my parents to visit English or Scots settlers, railway families or farmers; all part of the legion of 'uncles' and 'aunties' that children acquire among adults' friends. Most had died, some had moved; but they were not of my concern any more.

The concern for saving 'disappeared' persons had taken first place. Too many people had 'disappeared'. It became a priority to find out where they were, how many had died; there was urgency to compile a record of the dead and missing, the need was for faces, fates, names, ages ... before terror, and fear, wiped out all trace of them. We went by bus, by train, or I went alone, or with the editor in his car; we found others to check for us. The international news agencies – Associated Press, United Press International, Reuter – kept their own 'score card'. We checked ours against theirs; they read ours. In that first uneasy month after the military coup, the danger of such an investigation was not too great.

When we could go no further, we tried the Roman Catholic Church.

I called a priest with a parish in Buenos Aires' western suburbs and asked if I could see him. We had known one another for some time and could trust one another.

When I arrived on the bus, he was waiting by a wire-mesh gate that led to a small garden overgrown with weeds. I had travelled over pot-holed suburban streets through working-class districts scarred by the refuse dumps of small factories – the industrial belt that encircled the city with the development of the late 1940's.

'Good morning, Father,' I said after he had bade farewell to two old men who had stopped to gossip about parish events. We shook hands and half embraced. He wore a collar, as a token. For many months he had only worn collar and cassock for Mass; it seemed safer to identify his activity through more conservative dress now. He had been a member of the Third World Priests' Movement, depleted by a succession of murders committed by gangs of bigots, who opposed the social justice section of the church, started by eighteen bishops some years before.

We were friends; at least, I thought so. We did not see one another often; but we could talk; we sometimes lunched together; he sent people to me for help; I sent others to him. He had told me once quite frankly that I was a 'lost soul'. His religion could argue with irrational members of his church, the extremists and atheists; but discussion did not come easily with an Anglican turned agnostic who claimed to hold a strong respect for Catholicism and had married a Jew. Such wishy-washy liberals he found it a challenge to communicate with.

In his office he offered me wine, and his housekeeper brought two large cheese sandwiches. When I asked him for help to trace 'disappeared' people, he produced a few more names and numbers to add to the newspaper's growing list.

'Is the secrecy such that nobody can be found ever, Father?'

'It is not so much secrecy, as fear. We know some things. There is a priest not far from here who has confessed people before their execution. There is another in Córdoba. But if I approached the one near here, he would report me as a bad Catholic and a bad priest. They are convinced that they are saving the souls of Marxist heretics. Would you publish the names of all the police stations that have given you names and figures?'

I shook my head. 'I even tried to approach the armed forces chaplain. As a friend, I mean.'

'You would have him as a friend! That bloody old reactionary. Well, what did he say?'

'He gave me less than the police officers, less than you. Not even a word of comfort. He just said that this was a crusade against evil and that I should pray for the government's victory.' I felt embarrassed. 'He helped me get out of national service after my father died ... I had to go to him for help now; he was the only friend I could find in the hierarchy.'

'Oh, all right, stop apologising,' the priest said. 'It is interesting. He helped you, a Protestant...'

'Yes.'

'He thought he could convert you. Then you married a Jew...' He let out a short cough, then shook for a few seconds as he laughed silently. The *monsignor* and I had exchanged Christmas cards for many years; I had visited him once a year and sent him a copy of one of my books. In two recent sermons he had said Argentina was cleansing itself through the blood shed by the armed forces.

'The Bishop's evil and my hypocrisy will assure us a good roast in Hell. Your God will make sure of that, Father,' I said.

'He is still our God, not anybody's in particular. Come...'

He led me along a passage with coat hooks running the length of both brick walls, which needed finishing. We entered the empty church near an austere altar; the kitsch emblems of religion, silver-plated metal and plaster images of suffering dolls, stood in nooks and windows around the altar. Two low clerestory windows provided enough light to read by only in the brightest hour of the day.

He knelt in the front pew and faced the altar, inviting me to kneel with him. The church was empty; not even God was in it, turfed out for not providing enough answers to too many searching questions.

'God is not here, Father.'

'Speak to Him and perhaps He will hear you.'

The priest started a recitation of the Lord's Prayer and I looked around.

'Oh, Lord, we beseech You, help us in our search for the *desaparecidos*, Grant us the privilege of survival to help them. Help my brother compile a list of their names so that our children and their children will not forget...'

I stood. 'God can't give us that, Father. That's cheating.'

'Kneel and pray,' I was ordered.

'What for, to whom?'

'Pray with me, please,' he said.

I refused. 'God won't help us now. He is helping the other side. We don't stand a chance.'

I had started my protest in a loud whisper. As my voice trailed into a squeal, my cheeks were flooded with tears. The priest embraced me. Slowly, at first, rubbing my back with one hand; then he tightened his hold. He was a little shorter than I and his embrace was awkward. 'God will help, you will see.'

He led me out of the pews and back to his office. I gulped down the wine he poured into my glass and apologised repeatedly. If I had to describe the scene, I would call it poignant, even if I would always know that my tears were hysterical, the expression of my incapacity to overcome my frustration and fear. I left in a hurry.

The priest was murdered some time later. He was dragged out of his bed and shot in underclothes in a field in front of the church. Government sources let it be known that he was suspected of being counsellor to Leftists and that as a member of the Third World Priests' Movement he had aided guerrillas by preaching subversion. Death in any form is undignified; the lack of dignity seems even greater when death comes in underclothes in a field full of rusty tins and hedge-clippings.

'Oh, Lord, grant us the privilege of survival...'

8

PUBLISH AND BE TERRIFIED

June 1976

The conversation was about people who had disappeared. The number had become even more alarming.

'Will you report that Haroldo Conti was picked up yesterday?' The question was flung at me by one of the group. About twenty of us met once a week for lunch. Most were genuine journalists, a few were stooges who reported their conversations to military intelligence, and three were members of the military government.

The question was not an innocent enquiry but a challenge. It was also a way of announcing the abduction. They waited for a reply, aware that the *Herald* was the only paper in Buenos Aires that might report such an occurrence. They were professionally irritated by our daring, but convinced that we worked in the interests of some obscure but influential foreign power. They publicly admired our style and were privately contemptuous of it. Or maybe it was vice versa: it did not matter; either way we did not have their support when we needed it, but had their begging when they wanted ours.

The waiter came round with a bottle of red wine. I ordered my usual steak and mixed salad.

'Come on, *inglés*. Are you going to say anything about Haroldo?' R had made the challenge in the first place. Politically, one million miles separated us: I was a woolly liberal; he, a nationalist by his own definition. I preferred to call him a liberal nationalist, so as not to have to include him, a friend, in the sweeping generalisation, made by Jorge Luis Borges, that there was no such thing as rational nationalism. R had retorted that there was no such thing as a rational Borges.

But Conti was our friend.

I hesitated.

I did not know that Conti had been kidnapped. It was embarrassing; journalists do not like to admit that they do not know about an event.

It was, however, professionally expedient to avoid the usual hypocrisy; admitting to knowledge of 'disappearances' aroused suspicion about special contacts and informants.

I had last seen the novelist, Haroldo Conti, in February, one month before the coup, in the offices of a literary magazine whose editors he was berating for their refusal to publish an item with a strong political content. His girlfriend, Marta, some years his junior, had been prominently pregnant.

Some said that she and the baby had been sleeping when the flat was raided in the early hours of Wednesday; others said that she had been away.

There had been another man in the flat with Conti. R said that this other man was the person really sought by the raiders, because he was a member of the People's Revolutionary Army. From several throats rose a slow 'Aaah...' in explanatory acceptance. Conti could have expected no better if he harboured Marxist extremists. The momentary conscience prick had been relieved. Conti's sympathies with the ERP had been known. That did not seem to justify taking away in the night one of Argentina's and Spanish America's leading novelists. But he had another man, a member of a terrorist organisation, in the flat; and that adequately explained the incident.

R turned to the presidential press director, a former naval pilot, who as a liaison officer had been involved in the conspiracy which had led to the March *coup d'état* – infiltrating journalistic circles and planting information. R told him that Conti's flat had been looted by the raiders.

'They even took the barbecue set from the balcony.'

The government press official said he would make enquiries when he returned to his office. I wondered whether we would dare publish any of this. I asked more questions but there were no more answers. Nobody knew anything else.

R again addressed the press director. 'You people have really put your feet in it this time. Fancy picking up a man like Conti. The whole international solidarity set will be on your backs. In a few more hours Sartre, García Márquez, Amnesty ... will be showering Buenos Aires with messages of protest.'

The press director looked a little perturbed.

Haroldo Conti, in his early fifties, was a well-known writer, with book awards won in Argentina, Mexico, Cuba and Spain. He was controversial, despised for his political sympathies by the establishment press, but of some international renown. The press director repeated that he would do all that he could to find out what had happened. We believed him. Our capacity for surprise had not yet been saturated.

He looked at me: 'Publication of these things is forbidden.' I hesitated, about to nod acknowledgement; if I agreed in front of so many witnesses, I would have no excuse later. So I only raised my eyebrows. It was meaningless, but journalism, like politics, seemed full of meaningless gestures – private excuses for public impotence. Later, when trying to write something about Conti's abduction, I would tell myself that I had never acknowledged that publishing this was forbidden by military regulations. It was rather like making a promise with fingers crossed; the act was worthless beyond self-justification.

The press director was not satisfied with raised eyebrows.

'The ruling is that these things must not be published. You publish and there will be serious consequences,' he warned. It was a threat, to be taken in those terms. The problem with threats was that they were humiliating.

'I think we'll report Haroldo's story,' I declared.

The former naval pilot glared at me. He held up his hand, the fork waving between thumb and index, in a move that meant 'Just wait!' He claimed to have prevented closure of the *Herald*, when our reports of the raid on the *Siglo XXI* publishing company included a mention of the fact that security officers had stolen cash and foreign currency in the till. He had come out in our defence, he said.

I thanked him for his intervention. He changed his voice to warn that the military government was not worried about its image abroad; after all, had not a young Swiss correspondent of Berne's *Der Bund* been arrested on 19 April because of his interviews with Chilean refugees? Was he not expelled a few days later?

Yet nothing had been done against us...

I thanked him again; but he was not to be mollified. The *Herald* thought that it deserved special treatment, he sneered. A few days before, he had politely called to hand me a slip of paper, without any letterhead or authorising signature – thereby disguising the fact that it was a notification of official censorship – that read, 'As from today, 22/4/76, it is forbidden to inform, comment or make reference to subjects related to subversive incidents, the appearance of bodies and the death of subversive elements and/or of members of the armed and security forces in these incidents, unless they are reported by a responsible official source. This includes victims of kidnappings and missing persons.'

Instead of accepting such a notice as a licit course in anti-terrorist warfare, the *Herald* had run it as a strap across the front page. Only one other paper had mentioned the notice. The naval officer claimed that he had spent the weekend after that article trying to convince his superiors at the Public Information Secretariat not to close the English-language paper.

I reminded the Press Officer that I remembered that day: 'The newspaper *Clarín* ran a full page feature telling its readers that there were no restrictions on the press in Argentina.'

It had been irritating of *Clarín* to run that feature. I could not criticise the paper: it had been raided by political thugs in September 1973 and the offices damaged by petrol bombs. Among other results, one of their staff was still undergoing psychiatric treatment three years later. The bally-hoo of press freedom lost some of its momentum in such situations. Principled opinion dies quickly.

The press director was indignant. 'There is no censorship.'
The tension generated by his annoyance was broken by his
remark; several men laughed. The outrage of such a statement
and his temper sounded – as anger often does – extremely
comical. As the laughter quietened, he too smiled knowingly.
The conversation moved on to other topics. At the end of the
lunch we all parted on friendly terms, as usual.

Censorship, without any legislation to rule it, was spreading. The immorality of self-censorship became less reprehensible with the growing number of journalists killed. Papers did
not report arrests, deaths or 'disappearances'.

The press had published several congratulatory columns
about a public burning of books by a paratroop regiment
commander in the city of Córdoba. As several tons of porno-
graphy and politics confiscated from Córdoba book stores
and homes had gone up in smoke on 29 April, pyromaniacal
hysteria seemingly had been unleashed. Frightened families
burned every text in their possession that had a hint of left-
wing politics. Hugo, a poet who came often to share a cup of
coffee in my kitchen, had been away all that week. On his
arrival home he had found a tearful and apologetic wife...
He came to see me. He bashfully asked for the return of two
volumes of his poetry which he had inscribed to me. His wife,
in a panic, had burned many of his books, including his own
poetry. I ceremoniously counter-inscribed his own volumes
to him.

At about that time, we made belated enquiries about the
detention of a novelist, Antonio di Benedetto, arrested in
Mendoza immediately after the March coup. He was fairly
well known in West Germany in translation, but his tortuous
style had not made him a household name in Argentina. He
had been correspondent of the Buenos Aires newspaper *La
Prensa* and deputy editor of a conservative newspaper in Mendoza. His arrest had come as a surprise in literary circles; politically, he was a cantankerous reactionary. Our enquiries
found an answer from the Argentina Centre of PEN, the writers' association, one of whose committee members informed
us in great confidence that he had been found to be the ideolo-

gical mentor of a guerrilla network operating in Mendoza. On the other hand, a friend had told us that the arrest was the result of a private squabble with the Mendoza police chief, who had seen a chance to settle an old score by framing him as a leftist in the early hours of the coup. Such labels were difficult to remove. He would, however, be freed without charges or trial eighteen months later.

Censorship, in its widest possible sense, took many forms.

In June 1973, hours after the shambles and shooting that marked Juan Perón's return to Argentina from exile in Spain, a man at the door of the Social Welfare Ministry had boasted that he and others had taught a lesson to the Marxists, who had attended the reception for Perón, by killing them in large numbers. They had hung their enemies from trees and run sharp *tacuara* canes through their hearts. They had beaten them with chains and kicked in their testicles until their crotches were a bleeding pulp. *La Prensa* had identified the boasting man as the chief of protocol at the Buenos Aires town hall. The *Herald* also quoted him. He had denied the report and threatened to bring government pressure on us. We published a two column apology and I crawled to the town hall to add my personal regrets. Some months later, at a cocktail party, I heard the same man, who by then had moved to a post as public relations chief of the government news agency, boast of the same murders, in the same words.

Censorship took so many forms.

A politician friend told me that his faction had once decided to plant a bomb in my desk. It was to explode as I opened the bottom drawer. It was a very casual piece of information, casually delivered as we sat sipping whisky. His political aides knew my desk and what was in the drawer: dictionaries and a spare neck tie. The desk was by a window so that I would be blown out into the street below.

'Why?' I asked, with an unbelieving smile; the kind of smile that covers slow reaction to circumstances.

'Because of the Naipaul article. It said that Evita Perón liked cock-sucking. You people say a lot of things, but there are some you can't say.'

We had serialised *The Return of Eva Perón*, by V. S. Naipaul, from the *New York Review of Books* and one paragraph, almost unnoticed in the wealth of comment, said, 'She was the *macho's* ideal victim-woman – don't those red lips still speak to the Argentine *macho* of her reputed skill in fellatio?'

My friend's faction had decided that I had been responsible for the publication.

'But we decided later that you had done a few good things ... such as writing fairly about us. So we cancelled the order. Really, nobody would have given a damn if we had killed a journalist, except other journalists, and then they would have forgotten. Oh, it is bad for propaganda, of course, killing reporters; but it does not matter for very long.'

Dear Naipaul, who had asked us about Argentine politics while researching his article, very concerned with making metaphors sound right, he had unknowingly nearly got me killed.

Censorship did not need legislation.

After our weekly lunch, in the offices of *Crisis* magazine, where I had last seen Conti three months before, his friends discussed his abduction. His girlfriend had been to the magazine, but had added few details of weight to those already known. His sister had been there and it had been for her to file a writ of habeas corpus. His friends pleaded that I should not mention Haroldo's political sympathies on the grounds that it might damage him further. It had not struck them that whoever had picked up Conti knew his politics well enough to plan his abduction.

At the *Herald*, the editor decided that before publication we should await a copy of the writ of habeas corpus which was to be brought by Haroldo's sister. Since the 22 April notification that we could only publish information emanating from a 'responsible official source', we had decided to assume that a writ which had been entered in a federal court and had the stamp of receipt was an official source.

As more people came to the paper, complaining that lawyers would not handle their cases because the Interior Ministry asked the courts for the names of the defence counsels (and many lawyers had 'disappeared' or had died soon after being named), we became experts in writing the text of writs and advising on what courts were on duty.

But our requirement of a copy of the writ of habeas corpus was just another fragile journalistic safeguard. It was a legal resort to calm our own fears. Like other forms of justification, it could easily be invalidated by a raiding gang.

The editor did not hesitate in deciding to publish the Conti story and ordered the news item to be written in advance of the arrival of the writ. He was becoming impatient with our bureaucratic invention.

The world at large – apart from kidnappers, friends and journalists – learned of the abduction of one of Latin America's most popular 'new wave' writers from the *Herald* next day. The news item gave as its source local writers' societies. We could get away with that: I was a member of a subcommittee at the Argentine Writers' Society. I felt that they would have to be alarmed.

It was an excuse, again. Such justification was fictitious, just as reporters cheated themselves into a sense of safety because they peppered their papers with 'alleged' and 'reported'. We were protected against nothing.

We were left to wonder, and fear, what form the pressure would take. We would hear later about one naval captain who had resisted the demands of a colonel to close us during the weekend...

How would pressure come? It took many forms: the threatening letters – a sixth sense told us at a glance if they were genuine or not. The former we published, the latter we threw away. The telephone calls with obscenities and threats were a daily occurrence. On the days when there were no letters or telephone threats, we wondered why they had not come. They did not instil fear, but a dreadful tiredness. We became weary trying to disguise the threats from one another, attempting to ignore so many assaults on individual intelligence.

At night, in bed, there was time to wonder how punishment

would come.

We heard several rumours that the newspaper would be closed. People encountered in the street sucked in their breath and wrung their hands. The head of the press department at the Interior Ministry called repeatedly to tell us that 'I am a journalist too, you know; I just happen to have a government job, but my heart is in journalism and as one journalist to another I'm telling you: the Minister is very annoyed with your paper.'

Staff at one newspaper tried to publish an article on Conti's abduction; but the editor scrapped the page – and some of the staff.

On 19 May our hopes rose for the safety of Conti, and for other missing journalists. The president had invited four writers to lunch and each was approached by other writers and journalists appealing for the safety of missing human beings. But nothing happened. Jorge Luis Borges emerged from that lunch assuring the public that the government was in the hands of gentlemen. Ernest Sábato, a writer I admired, made a blanket plea for human rights and was ignored. A third guest, the chairman of the Society of Writers, was inaudible for his masticating; and the fourth, a poet and priest (who had once taught Conti when the missing novelist had, in his youth, entered a seminary) expressed his personal concern for Haroldo with the hope that he would soon be freed.

Haroldo Conti has never been seen again.

9

THE LENGTH OF A DAY

September 1976

I sat up, bolt upright at first, then rested back on my arms with my hands on the pillow. My breath wheezed asthmatically, preventing me from hearing the sounds of the street, from where the screech of brakes had come, piercing my rest. I sat there for a few seconds, one foot on the floor. As my breath calmed and I could hear better, I got out of bed, muttering to my wife that I was going to the toilet.

I tiptoed along the red-tiled passage and through the sitting room to the front door, all the time straining to catch a sound from the street. I stood by the door; then opened the peephole and looked out. There was not a living thing to be seen in the night that surrounded the dark yellow glow from the street lamp; such a simple sight was relaxing. In a moment the relief was gone and I thought about what there might be beyond the hedges on both sides of the front garden.

The sound of brakes had apparently not marked the beginning of an expected raid. It must have been the overreaction of a late driver who had come too fast upon a dip in our street. In fact, there had not been a raid in our block. In recent weeks there had been a raid at a house round the corner, another on the next street, another at the apartment building on the main road three streets away, and yet another at a girl's house two hundred yards away. There had been the sound of gunfire on each occasion; but in our block there had only been two bombs until then.

I made my way through the house back to bed. I had walked the same route three times in the last hour of attempted sleep.

It was half past three. I lay awake wondering if they would ever come. And who would 'they' be? Police in uniform, with an arrest warrant on the grounds that I had been writing seditious articles? Or would it be a paramilitary gang, with orders to capture a 'dangerous guerrilla', so that there would be no doubt that they would enter the house shooting? At another time they might even have been guerrillas, annoyed at being referred to as criminals. But since the coup, guerrillas were in retreat.

I always thought that it would be the paramilitary gangs that might come. It was easy to blame such an unknown force, simpler to fear their brutality, and it required less intellectual effort to elaborate their composition.

Once I had been shocked to find that my old school chums, and the boys who had gone to the same teenage dances, were being recruited in equal numbers by the guerrillas and by the right-wing gangs. And I had been further shocked at myself because I could not disown any of these acquaintances, and enjoyed a drink or lunch with them from time to time.

In the crude ranking of political terror, there had once been an element of status in fearing arrest by the paramilitary gangs, more than by any other security group. And God forbid that anyone be caught by uniformed police, whom tradition charged with catching only petty thieves.

I was wide awake and listening as she snuggled up. She dropped back into deep sleep and with a sigh. My right arm went around her shoulders and I closed my eyes. This was the only time for peace, yet peace was remote, removed from the tranquillity desired for ordinary suburban lives.

She had probably got to bed only an hour before me. That was the end of her day, which had started at seven when the children got up for school. It had probably ended when she nodded to sleep while writing an article for her art column, or adding details to a plan she had been commissioned to do in her capacity as an architect, or pursuing any of several jobs, from translator to reviewer, that had become necessary. It seemed impossible to keep an economic level or make ends meet in a country which had one thousand per cent inflation.

But had it been the end of her day? Or, as the clock said, the start of another and her short sleep a mere break in endless days?

This exhaustion had made her miscarry two pregnancies. And we saw little of one another. I left the house in the morning and was not back until 3 a.m. I spent the daytime in search of freelance work, or in search of political gossip and contacts to take back to the newspaper at night.

Recently she had told me that if we had not had a third child, she would have started an affair, sadly maybe, but necessarily. The strain was too much for her. The days passed alone; the nights she spent wondering if I would come back and what might happen on the way home. Daily, I wandered about the town, looking for news, for events and circumstances that would tell me that exposure to the public was a form of insurance against trouble. It was necessary to taunt danger to be able to know its extent. I was aware that each daring sentence in the paper made me more of a personality, which I wanted to be.

It was not a 'happy' marriage any more; but the world about us would never have guessed it. The family was falling to bits with awesome ease and vanity prevented me from taking a step towards repair.

I got out of bed once more, not for any noise this time, but just to make sure that all was quiet outside. This time she did not stir as she must have become accustomed to the movement.

I waited for a few seconds in the doorway, looking at the fireplace. How lovely it was to sit by it with the children in winter, staring at the embers and spotting the many-coloured flames. My gaze moved to the front door, a thin plank construction in which the boards had shrunk letting through a crease of light. We had to get a new front door. She wanted a glass door, to bring more light into the room. I was not worried by the material to be used, as long as it looked solid. The four-inch-thick front and back doors at my father's home had given me a sense of security when I was a child. We might be able to install a steel crossbar, like the ones on the shutters to the garden. But I knew that no door was secure enough against attack; I might as well settle for the glass door that she wanted. Plastic explosives blew out the best fitted lock. The explosive was fixed over the key-hole like a plasticine hamburger, and detonated. There would be no refuge.

I found myself hoping that an explosion would not shatter any window panes, because of the difficulty she would have in getting a glazier. I hoped that the house would not be too badly damaged when they came. It was a futile hope, though; nowadays when they came, they looted, wrecked, terrorised. What was it like for a man snatched from his home, probably to be killed, certainly to be tortured? Did the mind keep control of the body? Did the heart beat to explosion point? Did panic take over to unleash screams, groans or hiccups? How would the children behave? Would they cry? Would they be harmed in order to harm him?

I looked up at the sitting room roof, the dark beams high up, the varnish shining faintly in a glow from the street lamp. This was the house we loved, and we never wanted to leave. My son had decided that we should buy it in those days when we were searching in La Lucila for property; our own house sold, and prices rising at one million pesos a week, or was it a day.

The children were cramped into one room, and there was still much to be repaired, as soon as we had a little more money. She had directed the changes and had furniture built specially to her design... Here we would live forever. The children played in the cellar or around the little swimming pool or on the woodpile by the barbecue range. On warm days we had tea on the small patio – lunchtime, in spite of the awning, was too hot – or we sat out there in the evenings with the strong sweet scent of the jasmin flower in November. Here, in this house, we had spent the summer of 1974–1975 with hardly any need for a holiday away, because of the happiness of the house. Here the world beyond the front gate did not matter...

I went to the front door and peeped out, looking past the low wooden gate into the quiet street. One of the neighbour's bodyguards sat on the front garden wall, smoking and occasionally muttering a reluctant remark to his mate, who stood with a rifle over his arm in the shadows of the garden next door: two unhappy sentries in the new and booming private army business. They were there to protect a junior manager of the local subsidiary of the Ford Motor Co. The Ford executives had been threatened by guerrillas. All the Americans who had somewhere to go departed, and young Argentine executives stayed behind to rapid promotion and their own fears.

I wondered whether or not to greet the bodyguard; then hoped that my peeping would not be noticed. The idea of calling the guard was not because the company was desirable, but for something to do. I often stopped for a chat with the guards, usually on arriving home in the early hours on the empty street. The guards gabbled about rat-catching, political developments, gunbattles in or near the neighbourhood and, in what seemed a dedicated promotion of the bodyguard profession, a run-down of the latest of the daily abductions of the government's political opponents. The guards claimed to have special knowledge. I usually tried to remember each incident mentioned in order to check on the veracity of the report next day.

The conversation usually ended with a search for ant tracks in the front garden. The guards would ask what I had been doing, what politicians I had seen. Finally, the guards would repeat previous assurances that as the neighbour of a person with guards, I need not worry about security thanks to them. The guards would often go into a long report on the times of call of 'the patrol', an institution never fully explained as to whether it was a police control of the private armies or duty officers employed by the bodyguard companies to make sure their staff were on the job. They liked to be mysterious about the origin of the car with the two men who sat, unspeaking, listening to the guards' report. The guards often had a yarn about other cars coming by and drivers pointing to the windows, or slowing down to inspect the front, and it was always about *my* house, never that of the guards' protégés. The stories gave the guards licence to put further questions about the possible political connections of journalists. It was a tortuous way of prying, and a dishonest one; but people had become accustomed to the need for prying. And dishonesty was a way of life.

I went back to bed and again put my arm around my wife. How long was it since we had made love? It seemed like ages; ten days, maybe two weeks. It was a long time for us. I had this problem now – often I could not be roused. We would lie together on the bed, my fingers searching her body. We kissed and petted; but it only needed the screech of brakes outside – because of the dip in the road or the corner ten yards on – to turn my mind to the sight of bodies by the roadside shot through by dozens of bullets. Love-making became an awkward process, full of interruptions, elaborate explanations and regrets.

My last conscious thought was to wonder if I would ever be able to get out of political journalism, a trap in times of crisis, because a writer is snared into the need to keep pace with the changing faces, methods and circumstances. I had walked willingly into such a trap because it contained the most fascinating ingredients of people, of power, of evil and corruption. On the other hand, it was becoming an increasingly dangerous occupation.

I often wondered how my own death would come, hoping that it would be swift and not at the hands of the sadists working for the government, or the ideological imbeciles attached to the right-wing gangs.

'One bullet will do, gentlemen,' I would sometimes call into the dark of Plaza San Martín on my way to catch the train home from the paper. One bullet from a .45 pistol at a medium range would be quite sufficient.

The alarm clock rang, and my wife swung an arm to the shelf above the bed to shut it off. I did not move and after a few seconds she slowly got up to get breakfast for the children. Another day in which I would not see them morning or night. But my guilt and the weight of anguish were defeated by the need for rest.

The day before I had seen the children, when the household was woken by the stammer of two machine-guns. With my son we had gone out into the garden to hear where the sound came from. It had been a brief gunfight a few blocks away. The sound, each shot a clap, with its own echo overlapping the next, had come clearly across the quiet morning.

This was a common enough sound in Buenos Aires, day and night. I seldom went to the scene of the battles, usually started in an ambush or at a traffic checkpoint. The damage and the blood would be quickly cleared. One point to the credit of the antagonists was that they gloated over their victories in communiqués or in coffins, not over the bleeding bodies on the street.

Once, in a taxi, I had been driven straight into a gun-battle on *Avenida* Maipú, near home, in La Lucila. I was surprised at how easy it was to get killed, how accidentally I had survived.

The taxi driver approached the avenue on a side road, one hundred yards from the site of an ambush. The corner had been overlooked by police and troops, and as the taxi entered the avenue the first shots were fired.

The incident had started an hour earlier. A woman at a house nearby, the wife of a chemical factory director, had answered a call at the front door to be asked by a young man if her husband was at home and how long he would be there. She had suspected a kidnap attempt and had reported the strange presence in the neighbourhood to the police. She had seen two cars, with several men and one woman, outside the house a short distance from the wide avenue.

A person in civilian clothes hailed the drivers of the two cars and motioned them towards the main road. They must have realised that they had aroused suspicion and tried to make a break. They made a dash forward, one car directly at the man who hailed them, the other across the forecourt of a petrol station.

Neither made it.

As the taxi was driven into the avenue, the driver and I could see one car, with three men and a woman, cut down the plainclothesman; but the car went into a spin in the centre of the avenue and stopped as the driver was hit by the shots from a dozen troops in a small truck, which meanwhile had been parked on the pavement. The other car reached the service station forecourt just as it was blocked by a police patrol car behind which were three uniformed police. The guerrillas' car swerved into a petrol pump and three men leaped out firing, to be cut down immediately.

'Look, look,' said the taxi driver, braking suddenly and pointing first at the troops firing on the car and then at a policeman, who stepped back from the patrol car, did a little dance, turned to show blood pouring from his throat and then stumbled and collapsed on the pavement.

The sound of shooting filled the air as machine-guns answered one another and mixed in belligerent chatter. From the taxi we watched without movement, paralysed by curiosity.

In ninety seconds the men in the two cars were dead. A policeman advanced towards the car in the middle of the road and the only woman in the group appeared to sit up in her seat; the driver was beside her, slumped over the wheel. She called out something – later somebody at the service station said that her shout was 'I am pregnant' – and watched the policeman walk toward her, pistol in hand. As the policeman reached the door he raised the pistol in his left hand. She lifted her left arm in a move to protect her face. She did not scream, yell or plead, merely looked at the man who was by her.

From the taxi we would always remember that wide-eyed look of calm and resignation; but maybe we would just imagine the details of the whole event because there were eighty metres between us.

With the pistol barrel almost inside the car the policeman fired once, and twice. The girl jumped once, and again, as if the car had gone over a bump. She breathed with difficulty, gasping, as the policeman stepped back from the car, putting the catch on the pistol. She shrieked an oath, coughed a mouthful of blood and rested her head on the stooped shoulder of the dead driver. In a few minutes she too was dead.

'Beasts,' shouted the taxi driver as a police officer approached the cab, an Uzzi machine pistol aimed at us. 'You shouldn't have killed the girl,' said the driver, choking. 'Shut up,' he was ordered. 'I know who to shoot. What are you doing here?' The officer knew the answer to his question. 'Do a U-turn here and get out. Let me see your papers.' The driver handed over his identity documents, an item more essential than money in Buenos Aires. Without papers a person was liable to arrest as a security risk.

The driver repeated what he thought about the killing of the girl, as the police officer checked the documents with shaky hands. 'Yes, poor little thing; but it is better this way,' the policeman said, as if talking about a sick dog that had to be put down. 'If they had arrested her she would have been killed under torture. Like this nobody knows about her, nobody hears about it, and the newspapers don't bother. Anyway, these people have to be killed; things can't go on like this.' His excuse for murder as a release from torture sounded so human, so reasonable, so immensely merciful.

The driver turned to me and parroted: 'It is better this way.' Then he pushed his door open and vomited his breakfast.

'That is all I need today. Somebody to vomit on my shoes,' the policeman shouted. When the driver felt better, he drove away.

As we left the avenue, ambulances were putting the bodies on stretchers, and firemen were rolling out a hose to flush the blood off the street and the pavement tiles.

That afternoon my son came back from school with two empty cartridges. 'Look, bullets,' the boy yelled, cheeks pink with pride. 'Some men were killed on the *Avenida* and my friend gave me these.'

She returned to bed when the children had left for school. We slept for another hour, until the maid arrived and prepared breakfast. As I had expected, she became depressed at my announcement of an early departure.

'I never see you now. When are you going to be at home

and not asleep?' she asked. 'I reminded her that we would be meeting that evening at a cocktail party at the Australian Embassy. It was not much consolation, but she accepted it.

We looked through the morning papers. She searched the art and cinema pages for news that would break the monopoly that politics and the dead had on conversation. On my way to becoming an inveterate defender of lost causes, and forgetting to fight my own, I searched the pages for news of individuals kidnapped or killed by 'unidentified groups of heavily armed civilians claiming to be members of one of the security forces', a blanket description of paramilitary raiders.

As we finished breakfast, the Ford executive's wife from next door came in. After a rushed greeting and a refusal of coffee, she announced rather breathlessly that she was coming to report that her young son had seen a car drive by slowly, and one of the four men in it had aimed a movie camera at the house.

A short argument ensued as we dismissed the possibility that the house filmed might be our own. We worriedly made each other responsible for being an executive in one case and a journalist with questionable political contacts in the other.

How did the boy know it was a film camera? It looked exactly like his aunt's. Where did the camera aim? It swept both houses as the car passed very slowly. The boy became a subject of close interrogation by his mother, neighbours and the guards. In his innocence he enjoyed himself as an instant celebrity. Finally, both women decided that their children would no longer be allowed to play in the front garden. Newspapers had recently reported that the front of several houses had been swept with bursts of machine-guns, fired from speeding cars.

Besides, my wife had noticed men watching the house. It went on, until even standing in her own kitchen caused her discomfort. The men spent whole days on the pavement across the street. Two doctors had their surgeries there and she assured herself that they might be patients, and that she could not suspect all the people who stood outside the house. The fear lingered, however hard her efforts to dismiss it.

A car drew up to the house as we saw the neighbour out. It was another reporter from the newspaper to fetch me for an assignment.

It was the old morbid subject again. Several days ago a woman had written to the paper. She had asked for the correction of a death notice in the social columns, because the name of her deceased son-in-law had been misprinted. She had addressed her letter to me because, she said, she had known my father years ago – when the old man had taken us as very young children to visit their farm on the Paraná river, north of Buenos Aires. Her son-in-law had been taken from his home in Zárate, where he worked at a chemical plant (as well as studying at night) and had been left dying, a few days later, by the road near San Antonio de Areco, a way inland from the riverside Zárate. He had died within hours, because his heart had given out from the beating he had received – his wife had been able to recognise him by the hair and the clothes, not by the face.

The woman who had written the letter had only given a post office box number in a village on the northern fringe of the suburban sprawl. Land had remained relatively cheap there and so gardens could be large. The old couple had moved there on retirement after selling their farm. It was not difficult to find the house, even with no more than the official self-effacement of a post office box. A few polite inquiries in the shops soon led us to the woman and her husband. We left the car on an earth track, an alley flanked by eucalyptus trees, deep privet hedges, and a thicket of cotoneaster. We crossed two fields of tall grass, walking through clumps of bushes in flower. The earth smelled damp and rich; the scent of leaves and flowers carried on the lightest of breezes which put music to the scene with a rustle of long grass. It was inebriating. The mid-morning sun was warm and our walk was a joy. For a while, we forgot our destination and the job. We sniffed the air like pups and skipped a little. This was W. H. Hudson's version of the lane, an idyll of light, scent and sound carried on the wind.

This was the soil that General John Whitelocke had given

up hope of conquering for the British crown in 1807, arguing in favour of his surrender to the leaders of Buenos Aires. 'The more the soldiers become acquainted with the plenty the country offers and the easy means of acquiring it, the greater will be the evil, as the temptation is irresistible.'

The woman was glad to see us and with her husband launched immediately into physiognomic assertions, comparisons with my father and recollections of my sister. We were taken into the house, which, though the couple had been nearly forty years in the country, still had the mark of an English home, with that special colour of the wooden shelves, the smell of the polish, the brasses, the mat under the vase. They were grateful for the visit and were prepared to tell their story. But it was not for publication prior to consultation with their daughter and her two teenage children.

Two weeks before, their son-in-law had been fetched at about 2 a.m. by several men in dark casual clothes. The visitors had been polite and had told him to wear warm clothing. They had carried rifles and searched the house, but had not bothered with two shotguns on the sitting room wall.

The family had not heard of him again until he was found by a lorry driver, lying by the road. He had been taken from his home because his name had been in the address book of a guerrilla killed in battle. The man and the guerrilla had studied together, for night school exams. Several other fellow students had been picked up that same night, but all had later been freed. They had been held in some sparsely furnished offices on the banks of the Paraná river. They had known that they were near the river by the smell in the air, and by factory sirens from a metal works on one side and a meat packing company on the other. The students had assumed that they had been held at a navy depot on the river; but they had not seen it because they had been taken there blindfolded and had remained blindfolded throughout.

His fellow captives had heard him deny any connection with guerrillas. Whoever had beaten him had overdone it.

The dying man had been dumped far away so that he did not die on his captors' hands.

The father-in-law said that whatever the evidence, his daughter's husband could not be brought back; so he was putting the past behind him. The woman said that she had her suspicions based on the stories of the students. But she could not believe that the police or the navy were involved in the death of her son-in-law. If she accepted that, too many other life-long beliefs would have to crumble too. She was too old to accept such a change.

A few days after the death, leaflets proclaiming the man a martyr in the guerrillas' cause had been distributed in the factory in Zárate, where he had worked. The leaflets could have come from the guerrillas, intent on bringing down the family of the dead man with their carelessness; or from the man's captors, if they were members of a security force, bent on covering up their brutality. The employers, a US company, did not believe that their former employee was connected with guerrillas; but they were not prepared to state publicly their trust in the man or to question the armed forces. Times called for a low profile. They would help the widow and her children with cash, employment and education grants; but they would go no further.

As we drove back to Buenos Aires, my colleague remarked: 'This one we found because of a misprint in a death notice. I wonder how many more we'll never hear about.' (A week after our visit, the old woman telephoned to say that the family had been advised by their parish priest that not a word should be printed.)

The car left us at the door of the Andalusian club on Lima Street where we lunched most Thursdays with other journalists as well as politicians and several air force and navy officers. The number of officers seemed to grow each week.

The lunches had been a fixture for years. As the political crisis grew, and censorship intensified, the need for a clearing house for rumours, for the evaluation of stories, leaks, clandestine information and corruption reports became more pressing. We had made the Andalusian club our permanent meeting place.

A man, sometimes alone, sometimes with a guest, usually

took a table nearby and watched the meeting. The naval officers had once said that he was an army major attached to the State Intelligence Service. From then on the man was greeted on arrival and departure amid conspiratorial hilarity. That day, one lieutenant said that he was about to start his own importation business. On one or two occasions that lieutenant had mentioned the names of friends of his who were involved in the post-coup looting and abductions against leftists. Now he said that he could not turn against friends of a lifetime just because he hated some of their practices. So he was leaving the force.

Those lunches were a civilised way in which to watch and hear of Argentina's political filth. We discussed in a friendly manner the horror that was sweeping Argentina. And the greater the detail, the stronger the bond between us. This camaraderie created an element of tolerance and understanding which could be invoked in times of difficulty. Principles were admirable; but in politics they did not prevent arrest or stop bullets or win favours or give advance warning of a predicament. That was what contacts were for. Contacts could be asked for favours in the knowledge that they would be done. The debt of a favour was always honoured.

In the evening I met my wife at Retiro Station before going to the cocktail party. She asked if M had telephoned the paper; M had been very guarded when he had telephoned her at home. Yes, M had rung to say that his girlfriend had been picked up at the school where she had a class. What could be done? Nothing, except report it in the paper and knock on every door. The cautious telephone calls to the house and then to the paper, little pleas for help, were a daily event. Just as were the threatening calls on the paper.

How I wished that I could answer the telephone as had a friend when callers threatened to bomb a magazine and kill the staff: 'The threats office is only open from 10 a.m. to noon.' Of course, the friend's knees melted after that and he could not move for fear.

My wife said J had telephoned to say that he was leaving his home and newspaper job in Buenos Aires to go to Paris. There had been no letter, no threat... His flat had been searched by police, who had taken away his files.

'Isn't it time we left too?' she asked.

10

EXILE

September 1976

Victoria Station, Saturday. Struggle to get the children, cases, boxes, bags, dolls, off the train. Ahead is cousin Liz, waving, looking so lovely, so human – Laforgue comes to mind: there are three sexes, 'men, women and English girls'; cannot remember if he was trying to flatter or deprecate. Behind lies an overnight journey from the Gare du Nord, and far further back is Buenos Aires, left behind in a discreet hurry. My sister went to the airport convinced that she would not see us in years. My mother-in-law had dragged about a huge bag filled with disposable nappies, convinced that there was no such useful commodity in Britain; equally sure that our departure was for good, that we were lying when we said we would be back in a year. We were escaping just as she, in 1934, had fled her German-Jewish home in Warburg and gone to Argentina.

Every inch of a small Japanese tourist in front of us is searched by an officer with the polite indelicacy of the civil servant. We are waved by, thanks to the precaution taken by my father, a Scots immigrant, of registering me at birth at the British Consulate in Buenos Aires, thereby giving me the privileges of dual nationality.

Outside the Customs, the grey sky looks uncertain. We left Buenos Aires four days ago, on 21 September, the first day of spring, and have arrived in London four days into autumn. Books are being written about the worst drought in the century, which is ending with a drizzle. Young ladies have begun to wear cardigans over bra-less blouses, thus detracting from the pleasures to be obtained by the underdeveloped gloater. The tourists of that summer had reported that English women had beautiful nipples.

We are not exiles; take note. There is a British passport to prove it, even if birth and a lifetime far away may deny it. I am at Victoria Station to do Britain a favour, bringing my charm, my family, my experience, and no money. We have arrived with plenty of advice: speak English with a clear accent; don't go to the dentist; avoid the medical bureaucracy. Life is easier with a white skin.

We have arrived as the country is struggling out of the political mediocrity and diplomatic incompetence of the Harold Wilson government.

But that does not matter, we are in London, *City of any Dream* according to the title of a glossy book we have left behind. The hotel guide says 'Dogs allowed' and 'No children'. When the accommodation desk finds a vacancy for us at a hotel on Belgrave Road, my son is told to call his mother and father. The boy quietly asks us if we have brought any birds. There is puzzlement, impatience at the inopportune enquiry; finally, a closer questioning of my son elicits the statement: 'The woman at the desk said "Fetch your parrots."'

We went to live in Colindale, on a quiet tree-lined street that looked part of a set from a British film of the 1950s: empty streets, pretty with shrubs and garden borders. Nobody seemed to live in the houses.

As soon as we had an address, the literature of exiles arrived in the post – the exile magazines which asked for subscriptions and then faded after three issues.

We read them with the curiosity of the detached. We were visitors, not exiles, in London for only one year because we were sure it would then be safe to go back. It was interesting to be able to read the reports and reviews without the need to disguise them inside another publication. In Buenos Aires they would have been intercepted. In London we could enjoy the advantages of distance; the chance to read and sleep in peace.

Purging the mind of fear was a slow process. Fear had become a habit, a state each got accustomed to and reacted to by reflex. The car that coasted up to the pavement still aroused suspicion; a glance at the occupants, their faces, their number was part of an automatic evaluation of the danger, immediately dispelled by the recollection that the street was in London, not Buenos Aires, and nobody was after us. A car parked in an empty street was approached with care; one that was in darkness with two occupants inside caused alarm – but the occupants in outline turned out to be the front seat head rests. The sight of a policeman provoked a small, sudden intake of breath before the image was mentally processed and explained as a Bobby, the best in the world. Our son, on seeing a man standing at his front gate, asked if he was the guard, the bodyguard. It took time to overcome the patterns of fear that had become part of daily living, and dying. It was not easy to comprehend that we were in a country where the ordinary individual fears the tax inspector more than the police.

Insistence that we were visitors to England helped to convince us that we were only on a short stay. After all, there was nothing really serious to keep us away; there had been a brief arrest, a criminal trial for subversion, departure before the verdict of not guilty. Really, nothing that could not be overcome with the right connections.

The *Daily Telegraph* gave me a job as a sub-editor; the scullery maid of journalism and as boring. But it was Fleet Street, filled with its own myths, ale and name-dropping, and back in Buenos Aires it would help to put me in a special class of experienced professional.

Before the daily dose of fantasy was composed each night, the job left plenty of time for entertainment. Each in our family began to express preference for some part of London. My wife fancied Kenwood House and the Museum of London; my own choice was the British Library and the National Portrait Gallery; the children made their choices, which they enthused about for a time.

It was strange to discover on Fleet Street how conservative

was the entire British press. In fact, how conservative the British were as a nation. Scratch the surface of any Briton to find a conservative beneath even the most articulate Marxist.

At first it seemed bewildering that newspapers failed to record dates of events, which in most chronicles had simply occurred 'recently'. I was puzzled by such negligence. It took time to realise that dates were necessary in the region we came from, where records are either not kept or are destroyed. But, where matters are carefully recorded and annotated by civil servants whose work is preserved through centuries, reporting the time of day of each event is not immediately necessary, while the interpretation of events is.

One of the sub-editors on the *Telegraph* asked 'Have you had intercourse in London yet?' When the affirmative answer came, he asked, 'Do you foreigners wear pyjamas during intercourse? I mean, it must be pretty cold for you in London. Well, it's not too bad for a short time, I suppose.'

One day, some weeks after our arrival in England, a letter arrived. It was from L., a journalist who had moved to Montevideo after being abducted and held at an unidentified place of detention for fifteen days.

Among my captors was one who said he knew you and that they had you on their files. I was glad that you were far away and safe... Another accused you of being linked with those who attacked the Arsenal... They had us marked. They knew all sort of small details about us. I could not hide the fact that we had been working on a book, investigating the Ezeiza murders ... So they know that too. I am sorry, it is not good news. If you are returning at the end of a year, you had better remember this and take some precautions. The informers are everywhere...

My wife and I embraced, we cried a little... We were visitors no longer.

We left Colindale and bought a house in Golders Green, where the Jews are more Jewish than they are in Israel. We were accustomed to that, for the British in Argentina were more British than they are in the Conservative Party. I went to work at the *Guardian*, where the liberals are conservatives who counsel readers to vote Labour.

We began to wonder how we had come to be exiles in the land of my father and of his father; and of generations before them.

There was a sense of relief at the decision that had been taken for us. There was a feeling of abandon, the security of a stage overcome, mixed with an awareness that many frightening stages had still to be faced. It compared strangely with arrest. The mind wound down at the time of capture, in the knowledge of no longer being on the run, even if the horrors ahead would be evidence that there was no relief in detention. After the momentary relaxation, there would be anxiety.

Arrival in exile is a passage from hysteria to angst. The exiled journalist feels the angst from interpreting too many situations, sharing too many experiences at once, finally to decline into frustration and discover the impotence of exile.

For us, exile was, in addition, a middle-class privilege: the advantage of being alive, of having another country to go to; a comforting feeling. Comforting, even if it was full of distressing emotions, at a time when it was inconvenient to be emotional because such a state might distort an objective view of life around us.

At first it was difficult to understand the problems of exile, other than in terms of material necessities – cash, a house, a job, schools. Afterwards it became obvious that exile needed an ambience, the old friendships, the recollections and the links.

Being an exile meant noting something special in the ordinary. In England there are few South American exiles, compared to other European countries; we could observe all around us, while hardly being noticed ourselves. The English are the most tolerant, least religious people of the world, which makes them accept, in small measures, any idiosyncrasy as possible. Yet the English are without the concept of exile, except in the case of artists, and equate the exiled person with the immigrant, which means that the foreigner never has to be accepted as equal. The British can cater to exiled individuals, although not to communities.

Our South American contemporaries, who had left as the dictatorships closed in, chose Spain for ancestral reasons and language facility. Many had relatives and friends. Many went to Rome, descendants of some of the millions of Italians who had emigrated to Argentina in the first half of the century; a few went to Paris, where exile has its own literary and artistic genre, its political and social myths, and the mistaken impression that exile is catered to far better there than anywhere else. London harbours perhaps more foreign communities than any other city of the world – barring New York, perhaps, which shares with London an Anglo-Saxon disinterest in exiles. Paris, however, gives the impression of greater variety.

Some of the exiles from South America chose one of the East European capitals on ideological grounds. They discovered that left-wing sympathisers are not necessarily welcomed by Communist governments.

A few went to Cuba. But thousands chose Mexico City, Caracas or Lima, convinced that by staying in mainland America they were not moving too far from their ravaged homelands.

A number of exiles were professional failures, who assumed the role of the persecuted to win access to special allocations of funds, jobs and scholarships. There were others who had constantly to cross European borders to show that they were not resident where they lived; who relied on illegal employment or were at the mercy of office tyrants, from whom they begged for contract renewals and bureaucratic stamps to assure themselves and their families that they could breathe and could eat for another six months or a year.

They lived as suspects, humiliated by dependence, drawn to the dubious protection of refugee committees, solidarity societies, human rights organisations. There was a cosiness in the solidarity groups, which provided exiles with the fantasy that they had not been defeated. To be among people who spoke in the same tongue, could exchange anecdotes of friends, places, recipes, made up for the hostility of the alien activists who demanded political action.

There was the excitement of being able to tell personal anecdotes, with the added thrill of being alive to tell them.

Exiles passed around frayed cuttings, copying them, misquoting them in conversation, celebrating with frustrated irony each blunder of the military government. There were calls for unity among expatriates, yet the rhetoric of exile grew in bitterness, and the divisions grew as the chances of a return to the homeland became more distant. Each solidarity organisation demanded a commitment from individuals, forgetting that prolonged exile assured that nobody could be convincingly militant in a cause that was thousands of miles away. Many Latin American political exiles in Europe ceased to be militant, blaming distance, language, lack of time or the host country for a decline in interest.

Exiles came to our house and told us of dreams of their return, and we celebrated the dream with another bottle of wine. Those who had been political personalities in their countries made a pretence of being jovial, to raise the morale of others, while their own remained buoyant only in anger and vituperation against their victors. In quiet discussion their pessimism surfaced, for there was no early date of return. All were such wonderful people, but so ineffectual, unremitting in their denial of this and of its evidence: they were abroad, the others had won.

The dreams could turn into nightmares. As we looked back on what we had left, we dreaded the thought that faces and incidents might catch up with us. Recollections of the past and the fear of its presence in the future made adjustment to the present difficult.

However, exile became a state of constant discontent. It was not a physical state, not even one of the mind; it was, rather, one of memory. The present could not be lived without the supporting crutch of recollections, to create a fantasy of the past. The past had stood still on the day of our departure.

For some, memories were too personal, impossible to share with a husband or wife. Perhaps they could be debated with friends; but the friends were dead, or in prison, or in exile somewhere else.

Often nostalgia sounded like a whimper, the melancholy triteness of the dissatisfied. The complaints were self-centred, expressed by the self-indulgent. Memories became an exercise in narcissism. Some of us decided that exiles were the heroes of history because they had survived; forgetting that those who had stayed behind thought of us as anti-heroes, victims of our own fantasies, and reasoned that those who survived in their own countries were the real heroes. They had stayed and suffered the persecution and the silence, the ignominy of those forbidden to speak; yet had been there to bear witness ... even if later they might edit out what displeased them.

But exiles, wherever they were, had to face other difficulties. As the months passed, they found themselves losing touch with their children faster than other parents. The language of home became marked with accents or dialects or, in the places where the language was foreign, the native speech became faultier and patchy. The jokes, songs, music, that were so dear, so filled with remembrances, became lost on the children. The distinguishing asset that is another nationality was at first disguised, then mentioned to boast of a greater worldliness; finally used only to escape generalisations.

The reports, amusing ones, about exiles in other cities were frequent. Dr S, the well-known criminal lawyer, and his junior partner were posting bills in the streets of resorts on the Costa del Sol; while Mariano, who had always sold trinkets on city streets in Buenos Aires, had read and understood the new Spanish tax legislation and had established a rapidly expanding tax advisory service. Another lawyer had suffered embarrassment in Madrid: during an evening stroll near the Puerta del Sol, a car had backfired. He dived to the pavement and had to be assisted to his feet by two teenage *Madrileños* who did not understand why such a sound could be mistaken for a bullet. Estela, in Spanish-speaking Caracas, had sent her Argentinian-born children to the Argentine school, 'So that they don't lose the language.' The teachers were Paraguayan.

Ricardo, also in Caracas, made a habit of going to Maiquetía, the Venezuelan capital's airport, each day to meet those arriving in exile; one young man told him a tragic story: his brother had been killed, his father's house had been blown up by the army, his wife was pregnant, he had no money, no work and nowhere to sleep. Ricardo patted him gently on the shoulder: 'Well ... if you have any problems, let me know.'

Adolfo came to London from Granada with a bottle of Scotch to celebrate the fact that we were alive; reports from Buenos Aires had been muddled at the time of my arrest, and it was news of my death that had reached him. We celebrated, self-indulgence growing with the size of each measure poured.

It all seemed so difficult to explain in England. Buenos Aires is further away from London than Peking...

It took time to tune the ear to accents, even to the idea that English was spoken as the country's normal currency, and not as the preserve of a small expatriate British community which had looked on Argentina as another colony. For months, on bus or train, when out of the silence came the voice of a man or woman in conversation in English, it would make me turn to see who was there.

Much time was needed to adjust to a language which had at least six ways of describing a nullity: nothing, nought, nil, love, zero and O (the letter for telephone numbers). And the country's population is not referred to with the warmth of words such as 'citizen' or 'compatriot', but rather 'subject' and 'taxpayers'.

Jokes had to be lived with to be understood, however good the knowledge of English. The jokes based on television programmes or successful advertising required association. We thought that there should have been evening classes in slang, to help understand society's false modesty and its unfinished battle with obscenity, as well as the regional deformations that produced such edible items as 'sarnies'.

Graffiti opened a new world. Perusal of the walls of public

conveniences made possible an acquaintance with local inhibitions and prejudices. 'Rinse and return' was on a prophylactic dispenser; which also warned the unwary customer, 'I have never tasted such awful chewing gum'. 'Seven-up is great – ask Snow White.' There was 'Smash the IRA'; which made it just about the only place the English expressed concern about events in Ulster.

'Indifference rules OK' was scrawled as a misunderstanding of the fine art of understatement; there was almost an incapacity to talk without irony. There was understatement for any crisis. The bloodshed in Ulster was the 'troubles'. Years before, the counter-insurgency war in Malaya was an 'emergency'. Understatement seemed a form for preserving privacy, so strongly defended in Britain that it is part of a national heritage, though not protected by law. Both understatement and the idea of privacy conspired to disguise the barrier between the social classes. We were warned that in Britain there could hardly be individual success without the supporting elements of class and fortune, a public school education and a good university.

Everywhere there appeared to be a façade of harshness; underneath a depth of indifference. The foreigner met the politeness and understanding of the regretful executioner.

We began to belong in the city when we met acquaintances in the street, by chance. Our discoveries in the city's streets improved our knowledge of its half-secrets and half-truths. Prostitutes at King's Cross come in all shapes.

English weather, worse than anywhere else, precluded café life and reduced social communication and political debate. But we got accustomed to that too; to the use of public houses as landmarks for every direction; to the absence of toothpicks on restaurant tables, and the presence of ketchup pots; to vinegar on chips; to cooking in fat instead of oil.

However, it was not easy to forget the smells of garlic and onion and strong breath, part of a much longer residence in another place.

Soho and Smithfield provided all-night restaurants and

dawn-opening public houses. London never slept and it was beautiful to discover it so wide awake.

There was so much to learn. An aunt wrote and said never serve cheese at breakfast; at the theatre we were informed that the name of Macbeth should never be mentioned; and visitors should not whistle in the dressing rooms. Taxi drivers told their passengers that they had done their *knowledge*, which meant they had learned about the city in the lengthy test to gain a cabby's licence.

The English women looked vulnerable, in need of protection from the bullying of the nation's menfolk. English women looked lovely; they had large breasts and such beautiful complexions. In winter they all had red noses. They blamed Latin *machos* for sex. A lady called Mary Whitehouse – a self-appointed Inquisitor General into British morals – drew public attention to soft-porn programmes and publications.

In the English public house, male chauvinism was exposed. Women remained sober so that their men could drink to falling and then have the little woman roll them home.

I witnessed my first fight in London under the arches of the Embankment; watched my first Punks soon after midnight in Covent Garden, their hair cut and dyed in tufts that made them look convalescent from head surgery.

I discovered that British youth, as the rest of Europe's, had nowhere to go but into its own fantasies. There was no longer an Empire, no more colonies to explore, and not much employment at home. Those without the social break which a University offers before the endless monotony of undesirable employment could think of nothing but an empty future... The more enterprising went to teach in Central America, the less adventurous were reduced to being reduced. All about them was a class-conscious society, with little social mobility.

And still London loomed as one of the few vestiges of civilised Western society. William Morris's view of London and the Thames in *An Earthly Paradise* assured me of this. One of the daily comforts discovered was the sight of the London skyline rising out of the river in the Thames Television signal. From such a gimmick it was possible to derive the pleasure of being there. There was also an enormous inner glow imparted from BBC Radio 3, which closed down wishing me a very good night ... 'Sleep well – Good night...' I felt very snug.

On the BBC we heard poems read in a manner in which we had never been able to read them; stories that I had always wanted to read were read to me; literary traditions I had longed to know were explained to me.

This literary complacency was upset one night by the discovery, amid a large pile of rubbish on the Strand near Waterloo bridge, of a folder with poems – entries to a long-passed Cheltenham poetry contest. A pile of rubbish seemed such an inappropriate destination for so many expressions of feeling. The poems told of dying in Ulster, of Hampshire countryside, dying industries, life at a canal lock, and a northern housewife's problems. Never pass a pile of rubbish without at least a glance and a little stir. In the folder were letters in which someone discussed his choice of those who might be short-listed; somebody else asked for the source of a remark by Stevie Smith; Michael Horovitz, the poet, lamented that Beryl Bainbridge, the novelist, had called him 'Orifice', but denied that he had chased her about the garden.

It was a helpful introduction to the literati. It seemed an easier way to discover literary England than by mere bookishness.

New acquaintances showed their knowledge of Argentina with recollections of schoolday readings of W. H. Hudson. Graham Greene's *The Honorary Consul* was mentioned: the story being based on that of an honorary British consul, Stanley Sylvester, an Anglo-Argentine manager of an United States-owned meat packing plant. The Marxist group known as the People's Revolutionary Army had thought him a United States citizen and never really knew who it was they had picked up one quiet morning in Rosario.

Next came Morris West's novel *Proteus*, with the strange mixture of big business and human rights organisations. And then there was Paul Theroux's *Old Patagonian Express*, an ego trip pretending to be a travel story. I took a mean pleasure from countering, in conversation, his anecdotes, especially where he proudly reported meeting and reading to Jorge Luis Borges, Argentina's grand old man of letters. Borges, nearly blind, invited Theroux back on a second day to read to him. The North American writer was proud, unaware that the old man relied on his fame to get away with such invitations and thus secure a supply of readers.

It was paranoia that prompted such remarks, supplemented by name-dropping and the need to be known. One of the problems of exile is the passage from being well known in one city to being nobody in another. It seemed necessary to tell everybody how I had once been somebody.

11

RETURN

October 1980

Buenos Aires again. A city filled with lust. An invitation to be unfaithful to every love declared, to break every rule made, to go back on the very few principles held. A clean, yet filthy city, populated by the descendants of exiles, immigrants, outsiders all, who craved riches, the fortune promised in the New World and paid in non-voting shares. A people who cringed in the face of force – who had the genius to place this city on the edge of a plain and the banks of a silted river, and to fill it with the images of beauty left behind in the Old World. Buenos Aires had its own *belle époque*, and an accretion of styles dating back to a turn-of-the-century wealth extracted from the land: French, Italian, Moorish, mock Tudor, overrun by rats and the memories of rich Argentines at the races in Epsom and Longchamps; they sought the peak of fashion on Bond Street or Rue de Rivoli to take back to Buenos Aires. Georges Clemenceau wrote in 1911 that the city contained every style of architecture, but especially those that caused pain to the eye. Waldo Frank, the North American essayist, conveyed his muddle in an article in 1931: 'Houses are a chaos and a confusion; Spanish, Creole, Gothic, Baroque, Plateresque, Moorish, Neo-classical, Georgian, Victorian, French of all epochs, bungalows of southern California, streets tenemented like the East End of London, others like Menilmontant ... nowhere is Italian pastry-work more flamboyant, nowhere are hospitals, clubs, private and public mansions, more grandly expressive.'

Buenos Aires, 'the pearl of the (river) Plate' a tango called it.

A city with a genre of song dedicated to it. The tango was the social anthology of the city, a musical summary of its mores, of its ugliness and its beauty.

By night, as we came into land at Aeroparque, the flat city looked like a sparkling pancake; the fringe of the lights of Greater Buenos Aires faded into the blackness of the Pampa. The city was a beautiful, glittering, nervous sight.

A knot, which had been tightening in my stomach during the last week, now was at a taughtness that caused discomfort. The pain increased with the memory of the night before, of a kitchen in Uruguay, where all but a finger at the bottom of a bottle of whisky was drunk in celebration of the reunion with a friend, with his wife, with his children. The pain had begun to grow there, with the regrets and apologies.

'When they gave me the prod, I talked about you; perhaps I screamed about you and accused you of things; I am sorry. I asked them if they were police or terrorists and they said terrorist-police, laughing at me. I asked where they had taken me and they said to a rest home. They mocked. They promised that you would be brought to keep me company. Must you really go to Buenos Aires? Would you like me to go with you? I have been back twice for short visits this year. Shall we get you interviewed by a paper in Montevideo and publish a picture of you boarding the plane so that there is evidence that you were here? So that they can't *smoke* you...*

It had been so lovely to be there and talk and listen to a dialogue, until then reduced to the whisper of long letters which had to be given the memorised recording of distant voices. The crossing of the River Plate to Buenos Aires had then been twenty-four hours away; boldness had still been possible. There had been time.

The plane touched down smoothly; my stomach crashed in a blaze of twisted feelings.

The plane was half empty and the queue at the immigration desk was uncomfortably short. The policewoman at the desk was petite, elegant, almost approachable; she stacked the dis-

Fumar/smoke: to make a person disappear, vanish, to make him/her go up in smoke. *Chupar*/to suck, is to abduct.

embarcation cards passed to her by a smart young man – my first image of image-conscious Buenos Aires – who checked documents. Behind them in a doorway to a Customs recess, stood a short-unpleasant-looking woman. She looked clean, but coarse, graceless in the meticulous attention she gave her short fat hands; I kept wondering what there was in that room.

My passport slapped into the waiting hand; it was, thank goodness, perused with little interest – and a three months visa was stamped into it. I was being told by means of a stamp that I no longer belonged here.

The next steps were light – almost on air, stiff, quick in fear of being recalled – to a taxi rank.

Buenos Aires again, where life had begun and, until four years and one month before, had always, quite reasonably, been expected to end.

The exile's reunion with the city of the past is like the return of a divorcee to a former dwelling. In this corner that happened, and here this ... Yet nothing gives the feeling of belonging any more. Outside of the memory there has been no physical change; but nothing is the same. I check the telephone directory, but not even that offers an assurance of belonging: my name is no longer included.

The city is the same as four years before. The same spirit, which built palatial residences in the first decade of the century, is at work criss-crossing the city with thoroughfares to carry fast traffic into suburban oblivion.

At the Reuter office, where the staff turnover could be expected to have cleared all familiar faces, an unassuming entry is met by greetings of recognition.

'Oh, they let you in ...'

'You didn't have any trouble getting in, did you?'

'They didn't stop you, did they ...? No, of course not, things are better now.'

People, friends, insist on that, even if they know it is not true. They address the returning exile as they would a public meeting, with the pat answers of government propaganda, put-downs to any protestation.

I am back to the moral squalor of self-censorship and to re-crimination over the motives for departure.

'You left when things were at their worst...'

'We stayed and stuck it out...'

The Argentine military government's slogans inform the public that the seventies witnessed a war, a 'dirty war', but a war no less, and that the guerrilla organisations have been van-quished. The war is over. Yet there is no feeling, no political spirit of a war having been fought; no concept of victor and vanquished; only an idea of a small battered group which had at one time a terrorising hold on society which was broken by political and military persecution.

For those in exile, there is not even the romance of battles fought, even if lost. Alain Resnais, in his film *La Guerre est Finis*, explored the intellectual failure of the Left to see the Spanish Civil War in terms beyond an anecdotal experience; the anecdotes of combat and minor victories, narrow escapes and heroic defeats, all made the stuff of exiles' memoirs. There is none of that to be found among Argentines. Two small fac-tions of society, two elites, the armed forces on one side and the guerrillas on the other, have taken part in the fighting. And although it has affected thousands of homes, including those of innocent bystanders and minor sympathisers, the ma-jority of the population can look back unperturbed by events.

A few weeks before, towards the end of September, a Bri-tish army major general and university lecturer, who had spent a few days in Buenos Aires, wrote to a local newspaper and said, 'I have no doubt at all that, of those killed, the great majority were killed in battle, in a very violent war.' He had been writing about Argentina; as if he wanted a war. At least, the country has been spared that.

Every walk through the city is a renewed adventure. At every corner of the familiar city there is the risk of being run over by memories.

Departure, four years before, meant leaving most things behind: a job, memories, mother-in-law, books, and a house with all its contents, taking only what could be carried on a plane and the notes of a report, leaked by a police officer, of an investigation into the investments made by the Montoneros guerrillas.

The *Daily Telegraph* ran my article for one edition, then threw it out. A few weeks later the story broke: the Montoneros had given a fly-by-night banker 17 million dollars – the product of ransoms and extortion – to invest and administer for them. The banker had paid Montoneros a monthly interest with which to fund the wages of combatants who had lost their surface covers and to finance armament and equipment. The operation had been discovered when the banker had met his death in a plane crash in Mexico and four merchant banks controlled by him, two in New York, one in Brussels, and one in Luxembourg, had collapsed. Nearly 60 million dollars had been missing. The papers were full of the story then. So much for scoops.

The walls of Buenos Aires have been cleaned. In 1976 people were shot for painting anti-government slogans on the city's walls; the custom declined. The clean walls of Buenos Aires no longer record statements of revolution, threats of vengeance, party proclamations and promises. White walls are the sign of a silent people and of the order that bars them from shouting their sympathies in large letters. The public is at peace.

'It is quieter now. The city was cleaned up for the 1978 World Cup. You can go out at night without being afraid,' people assure me.

Events become nebulous; the mind closes to the idea that it was as much the security forces as the guerrillas who filled the night sky with the rattle of machine-guns; that no battle, not even the one the British major general wanted, was part of a straightforward war. A bomb could have been planted by an officer, who wanted to embarrass his superiors, who in turn wanted to put pressure on their commander, who wanted to discredit the government, which blamed the guerrillas, who claimed credit for one of their cells, which tried to contact the officer to pay him for more bombs... People can go out at night now, because some of the entrepreneurs in that chain of political corruption have been killed.

There is not enough money to spend to go anywhere at night. The restaurants and theatres that used to give Buenos Aires the most famous night life in South America are half empty; it is no longer possible to buy a book at four a.m. – there are no longer any customers at four in the morning. Even when customers are to be found on the occasional Saturday night, the books are not there: so many have been banned.

'Have you seen the musical *Evita*? Is it good?'
Answer: Yes to both questions. The air fills with the sound of Julie Covington's recording of 'Don't cry for me Argentina'. The musical was not banned; but officially discouraged. Tapes of the music were bought in London or New York and copied dozens of times to satisfy local curiosity. No house could be without one. Evita Perón in death had the acting career she never had in life – excluding her performance as a politician.

Streets hold the memory of winding queues that spanned the centre of the city as people waited to see the body, being rapidly embalmed, of Eva Perón. Jorge Luis Borges, in writings and interviews, ridiculed them later – and Naipaul would take his cue from there – but they were mourners who had lost a little mother. In another July, twenty-two years later, the streets had again filled with mourners, queueing to see the grotesquely bloating corpse of General Juan Perón.

Ana is in tears on meeting; she says that she had never expected to see any of us again. Jorge's embrace lasts for a long time, his smooth cheek very close, while his huge paunch keeps the distance; he rocks as he hugs me. At the *Buenos Aires Herald*, people wear suits, and shake hands when we meet; four years ago we drank to forget, and it required a decision to hit each type key.

How self-indulgent the exile feels; how self-centred and vain. Departure meant breaking from the village; but now there is the risk of antagonising those who stayed, by criticising their submission and endurance. Who had more need for allies and friends? Those who left, or those who stayed? Both needed so much reassurance.

'Well, you have not seen bodies all over the place, have you?' jokes the captain at the public relations office in the Libertad building, the navy command. He smiles.

'No. You have very good dustmen.'

The meeting is a result of an introduction arranged in London. 'We will do nothing to you. But we cannot guarantee your safety,' the senior naval officer advised. 'Do not tell anyone where you are staying.'

His words of caution force a change of abode every night.

Calle Florida, the most famous pedestrian shopping street in South America, looks like an elegant market place; foreign goods fill shop windows: import duties have been lifted. With the national airline office at one end of the street, and Harrods at the other end, Florida gives the impression of being a lane leading to a dream country of rich possessions, all behind glass and all within reach.

One game my friends and I used to play before, on *Calle* Florida, was to compete to see how many people we knew who were also walking along, wanting to be seen. There were ten points for whoever stopped and engaged in conversation with another pedestrian; only one point for a greeting returned; and points against, when a person did not answer a greeting or looked back bewildered.

On this street, Diego had once had his office. The meetings in his office, engulfed by the white leather upholstery and surrounded by fitted tanks with tropical fish, seem so near.

Of the nine who met in that office in 1974 to plan a magazine to be called *Puro Pueblo*, over half are dead. Diego is dead; so is a merchant-navy first-mate who had exposed information on the private deals and fortunes made by scrapping obsolete navy ships. Rodolfo is dead, shot in the face when his car was ambushed after he had left his office in the Chamber of Deputies. Brutal justice ... for his own oath of office had been, 'The blood that has been shed will not be forgiven.' He had been a brilliant lawyer; but like several of his contemporaries, he had put his brilliance in the service of a revolutionary fantasy that had death as its obsession. His political belligerence and style – and that of his contemporaries – had been foreseen with contempt a decade before by Witold Gombrowicz, a Polish expatriate writer living in Buenos Aires. Gombrowicz, in his *Journal*, had directed his irony at Mario Santucho, chief of the People's Revolutionary Army, with whom he played chess at the café Tortoni, on Avenida de Mayo. Gombrowicz had ridiculed the revolutionary politics upheld by Santucho: those politics took Santucho to his death in a gunbattle in July 1976.

There had been others at that meeting who have died or have gone into exile.

Ironically, their magazine, which only lasted about four issues, paid for by Diego and produced by his friends, advocated an end to guerrilla action and a critical support for constitutional government.

Most were leftists, convinced that there was a constitutional revolution to be made, unaware that the revolution they talked about was not understood by the public. The working class thought of revolution in the same terms as soccer, something to be enjoyed for an afternoon – perhaps a good brawl to get a few things out of the system – and after the event and a good meal, a return to work on Monday. Guerrillas and politicians on the Left never convinced Argentines of the need for a prolonged struggle to bring about change.

The men and women who thought that ideology could sustain them against any odds were, in all but a few cases, robbed later of such sustenance by the shock of the extent of human cruelty. Without the resistance that ideological commitment had been thought to give, many bent and broke. Leftist idealists, and the guerrillas they supported, had shown not how strong the insurrectional cause had been, but how weak was democracy. And the innocent victims numbered thousands.

Then came the time for all to wonder how to live with those who had really suffered; those who had lost their mates; whose children were no more than a memory snatched before dawn...

Parents became known as the kin of 'disappeared' people – the 'relatives' of those who had been defeated. These relatives could not mourn their dead; they suffered the added anguish of not knowing if the 'disappeared' were dead. The relatives had to pray at home-made altars, behind closed shutters, in silence, with dwindling hope.

The streets of Buenos Aires have many of these shuttered windows. Behind the shutters are memories, often kindled not into recollections of times gone, but into a fiction of continuing life.

One woman said that her son was still alive, watching her, spying on her in the street, never approaching her in his embarrassment at having been a *desaparecido*. She said that he was afraid to come home and was a tramp; but she could telephone him, she had a number at which he could be found... Urged to call, she said that she had copied the number incorrectly.

A mother said that she was sure her son might still be alive in a secret place of detention, in a *pozo* – a cell below ground level – but was equally sure that her daughter-in-law, abducted with him, was dead. The girl, said the mother-in-law, did not have such a pleasant character.

A middle-aged couple had sworn their children to secrecy about the 'disappearance' of their elder brother. Once a month, the parents wrote a letter to themselves, on blue paper, telling the news of an eldest son who was writing from Spain. They circulated the letter among his aunts, for they could not bear the embarrassment it would mean to the rest of the family to know that one of their nephews had been abducted by the security forces on suspicion of being a member of a guerrilla cell.

A father had paid a bishop – reputed to have 'occult' powers – a sum of money to establish spiritual contact with his youngest daughter, abducted for being a member of a progressive Roman Catholic self-help group. The bishop reported contact, though he could not reveal her place of detention. He encouraged the father to get her passport in preparation for an early release. The old man paid a police officer for the passport. He never saw his daughter, the police officer, his money or the passport. The bishop advised him to be patient.

H's partner at the law office, who distributed the magazine of the People's Revolutionary Army in the provinces, was pushed out of the window of a provincial police headquarters. It was not a long drop really – only three storeys. But he was semi-conscious after torture and they had no use for him any more. His body was never found.

The *Buenos Aires Herald* carried a report of a man who had to go to the Supreme Court for help to find his missing son. The young man's employers would not give any character reference; the father could not get any lawyers for none dared take up the case; and the matter had been delayed in a lower court on the excuse that the judge could not have photocopies made of the petition for enquiries – there was no copier in the court.

Mario, a friend, said that while he was in prison, whenever he demanded to be heard by a court, his interrogators would refer to the judges as condoms: 'We throw them away after use.' The condoms were displayed to show that they were there, but they were seldom used.

Mario knew. They had gone to fetch him at his house on the day of the coup, telling him they had to ask some questions about the newspaper where he was news editor. They had said it would only take half an hour. He had spent four years and nineteen days in prison; thirteen months of that time alone in a dark cell from which he was allowed out for only a few minutes each day for the quickest of ablutions. For companionship, he had only the infrequent visit of an army chaplain.

Many priests visited Argentine prisons – not all of them were good priests. One, on hearing the complaint of a prisoner in Córdoba that he had been tortured all day, expostulated: 'That is terrible; we had agreed that they would only do it for three hours a day.'

In the Coronda penal establishment, the chaplain never went into the solitary cells: he counselled through the peephole that prisoners should not masturbate.

Bad priests ... the mistake was, perhaps, to expect priests to be better men.

In Caseros, the priest interrupted the Lord's Prayer whenever an officer walked into the block. In La Rioja, the chaplain told an inmate who groaned from the effects of a severe workover, 'Well, if you don't want them to beat you: talk.' In Rawson, the Sunday sermon began: 'Dearest murderers...'

There were many decent priests, although most were silent, which in a way made them indecent. A few are dead, and are also silent. A number of priests are in prisons, as captives. Only a handful are outspoken in spite of the danger. They have no support from their Church leaders. The Church is still too titillated with sexuality and matrimonial morality to speak out on torture. The Church still thinks that it is evil to speak of a guerrilla, even a defeated guerrilla, even if mistakenly accused, as just another human being. One priest compared guerrillas to a cancerous growth. He forgot that cancer was produced by the body.

'You must not believe all they tell you nowadays about those things,' an old priest says. He had been my source for an historical reference years ago and I sought him now for a political reference. 'Time will tell who is speaking the truth. Time and God will help us discern...

'Otherwise we will all become too wild. I remember that I had a nightmare during *siesta*; one day when all the shootings were taking place, I dreamed that I had driven my van up to a traffic signal and as I waited for the green light somebody aimed a rifle at me and fired... In my sleep I did not ask God to assist me, I shouted: "Mother Whore, they've got me"... I spent the rest of the afternoon saying Hail Marys... I had to.'

He speaks into my ear, his face close to mine, 'What I am trying to tell you is that we all get overtaken by these things. The smell of gunpowder is inebriating. It is like sniffing one of those drugs that give people hallucinations.'

People prefer to forget. They cannot be expected to believe all the stories of private tragedies: belief became unbearable. The Uruguayan journalist, who was arrested in Buenos Aires so that he would not report his son's abduction by Uruguayan officers working in cooperation with the Argentine services, was hung by the wrists, his feet twelve inches from the ground. Electricity was applied to his body. If the wrists had slipped through the wire, he would have fallen, as others had, on a wet floor covered with coarse salt. People were dipped head first into large tanks of water until the bodies no longer moved. Others were pushed out of helicopters into the River Plate, their hands tied behind them with wire.

Wire handcuffs sometimes replaced the regulation service cuffs when captives were taken out of a prison or a police station on their way to a secret place of detention or death. One survivor had told his father of his panic when wire hand-cuffs were wound round his wrists. They left them on him for so long, they caused paralysis in one arm. They returned him to prison. Some weeks later he was shot dead in what was presented as an attempted escape.

In a secret detention camp in Córdoba, one girl of the Montoneros was tortured by electric prod and raped repeatedly by one tormentor, a captain, who each day selected her for his outrages. After days of cruelty he rewarded her with caresses, took her to his office and made love to her gently ... She became his mistress; she won her freedom that way.

Other women watched their clothes rot at the arm pits, their dresses fall away. Men felt the humiliation of smelling their stinking bodies and were hosed down by jeering guards – those were the only baths they got. Women peeled sheets of skin off their thighs, dead skin, killed by frequent application of electricity. Teenage boys and girls died slowly in tiny compartments, no bigger than small cupboards. 'A policeman threw water under the doors of one boy's cell so that he could drink it, mixed with excrement; it was all he had to drink ...' Why were such young people there? They had been taken from their schools when found in possession of gummed labels with revolutionary slogans. Others had joined the

Marxist-organised Guevarist Youth. The security services thought that such an association was not dangerous at the age of seventeen, but it could prove subversive in four or five years time. So they 'disappeared'.

'In June, the coldest time of the year, a group of soldiers came back to the Campo de Mayo garrison with two men in a lorry. They were left in the lorry for a week, tied hands and feet, hooded, wearing just shirt and trousers in freezing temperatures, with nothing to eat. Some soldiers smuggled *mate* to them. After a week one of them died: they took him to the ditch where they burn the bodies; it is near the firing range. There they had put a tank of aviation fuel and they burnt the people who had been shot or had died under torture...' A soldier wrote that to his parents.

It is best not to believe all that people say. People will forget; time will help.

Only if somebody writes this as fiction will it last, will it be believed. Journalism expires within twenty-four hours, and it is so easy to forget.

Dora was ordered to deliver Luis's car papers to a man who waited at a corner on *Avenida* Libertador. But she was not to stop, just to throw the papers in a plastic bag from a taxi and drive on. They already had Luis's car ... and Luis; his captors needed the papers so that they could sell the car.

In 1979, the government introduced a ruling authorising the kin of the *desaparecidos* to record them as dead when they had not been heard from for a year. Marisa's parents went to register her as dead to transfer the deed to her house to her children. They found the house had been registered in the name of a naval officer.

Some officers involved in raids had to undergo psychiatric treatment, made necessary by the lasting shock of what they had gone through, and by the fear of avengers in the future.

Every part, no, every corner, of Buenos Aires holds a memory of a friend or of a conversation; the sight of a face that can no longer be there.

At the police headquarters, the unmarked cars are still the

same – they look a little cleaner, better polished – now, however, they all have licence plates. Security is a licence plate on an unmarked police car, even if it is the false security of a useless and untraceable plate.

The empty Congress building holds recollections of hurried appeals and rushed signatures to secure releases or at least publicity of arrests.

A seat in the park in front of the Colón Opera House reminds me of the night I heard Joan Sutherland. I went with Pirí to hear my favourite *prima donna* and afterwards we sat in that seat in the park and stared at the Colón and argued about the difficulties of translating Dylan Thomas into Spanish. I should like to hear Sutherland again; I could even go to where Thomas lies buried; but I cannot speak to Pirí again. She has disappeared. The last anybody ever knew about her was from people who were later freed from prison. They said that they heard a guard shout at her, 'Hurry up, you stupid bitch . . .'

A wave of self-pity fills me with the thought that nobody cares any more; all those who 'disappeared' are being given up for dead. I stare at Buenos Aires through my past and feel the anxiety of being displaced. All about me people are trying to forget.

12
TEA WITH THE TORMENTOR

March 1983

It was the time of afternoon to stop for coffee – any friend's office would do for the company, rather than drink alone in a bar. I looked for the office of a former naval man, somewhere on *Avenida* Corrientes. He was in, chatting with another man. They were waiting for a third. It was the third, Lucho, who would take us deep into the nightmare.

The man who owned the office had been in the navy. A lieutenant in 1976, he had pulled out to start as a ship's chandler. He had left the service to avoid being involved in the terror then being planned. He would not pass judgement on those who had taken part in the horror. His departure made him decent.

His other visitor was introduced as Javier, formerly in the army. His full name was not given. It was not the casual manner of informality, but the protective reaction of the security-conscious.

My full name was given. The two men were young, their features soft, their appearance cared for. Appearance was, if not all, at least eighty per cent of a man's assets. Business had brought them together. I sat down next to Javier, an old fashioned wooden desk separating us from our host. A print showing a scene of Argentine *estancia* life, a calendar, and a coloured picture of the Sacred Heart were on the grey-green walls. I commended our host on the central situation of his office. He had done well during the monetarist madness of the military regime in the late 1970s, when imports were cheap. He returned the compliment saying he had read my writing.

The door opened suddenly and in came Lucho, the man who they had said would be interesting for his views on the 'dirty war' – the euphemism for the years of terror.

Our host offered tea: he had run out of coffee.

Lucho sat in a chair with its back to the wall and winced as he reached the seat; he straightened and removed a pistol from his belt. He laid it on the desk. The servicemen showed no reaction at the appearance of the gun.

We were not destined for small talk.

'I don't know how you can be on both sides,' Lucho said on meeting me, an Anglo-Argentine. His dark handsome face became hard, his eyes flashed hatred. Then the feeling receeded. Javier cut short further expression of emotions saying that he and our host had been about to explain Argentina's political situation.

Lucho sounded reasonable. He told of how servicemen had been ravaged by conflict. 'It's not a battle against a foreign enemy ... I am not saying that fighting foreigners is any easier; just that it is different. A *guerra sucia*, as we had, is a conflict where men are fighting people who speak their own language; it is a fight in the family.'

It should have been good reason for greater compassion, I remarked.

'On the contrary: family rows tend to be far more cruel. Close acquaintance eliminates the need for discretion. The toll on men's minds and livers is terrible. Once, when I went to the military hospital, the doctor said that the army had employed 150 psychologists in 1978 and 1979 to treat young officers who had operated against the subversives. I don't know if it is true. But when you are told something like that, there is always a root of truth in it. The young officers had to be taken care of, because not all could be allowed to leave the service. Some had to be promoted.'

'I presume you didn't crack under pressure,' I said. He reached for his pistol from the desk and stared at it as he turned it over in both hands. He spoke again.

'Now the problem is different. How do you negotiate the end of a civil war when there is no supreme victor? We beat them; but we cannot claim victory. There are political considerations. And if we have to negotiate the end of the past, we have to know with whom. We must know if the negotiators are strong enough. The talk of amnesty is the babble of imbeciles at the Interior Ministry; or maybe the command is flying a balloon. An amnesty does not end the shooting, nor stop the mad men who want to take revenge. You need to make a deal with political figures who can control the mad lads, the *loquitos*.'

'Did you crack?' I asked Javier. He hesitated and looked at Lucho, but saw no reply in the other's eyes. The conversation was moving close to a point I had sought ever since, three years before, a man had told me there were those who had cracked. He knew. He had been a presidential candidate in 1973 and was a former naval officer. He had spoken in anger, with sympathy for the officers who, in fear of reprisals, had changed their names and had to move out of the towns they had lived in for years. Marriages had broken, men had remained maladjusted.

Javier said he had asked for a transfer and had got it thanks to a colonel. 'There is a limit to the amount you can take, because, really one is decent. . . .'

Our host put four cups of tea on the desk.

A metallic snap caused a catch in my breath; then there was the slide of metal on metal and Lucho pumped the barrel housing of his .45 pistol, releasing a nine millimetre bullet. A magazine with four or five bullets lay on the floor. Without looking up, he studied the detonator on the bullet. He was playing a military dare game. The snap sound had been the hammer on the bullet, the hammer pulled back to see how much of a mark could be made on the detonator without the gun going off. He looked up, only in part pleased with the effect.

'Did you enjoy your job?' I asked. He started, looked surprised, then half closed his eyes until his face looked cruel.

'At times,' he said casually. 'At times, but it was not a matter of liking. I had my orders. I obeyed them. We had to rid the country of subversion and we nearly did it . . . nearly.

If it had not been for bastards like you, yes, in the press, in Europe, where you had run away and filled the papers with anti-Argentine propaganda. . . .'

My stomach made a sound of rushing fluid in a suddenly unblocked drain, then I broke wind silently . . . a premonition of panic. I raised my cup of tea and sipped slowly, to cover my face. My thoughts went to the Czech writer, Ludvik Vaculik, who once wrote a story called *A Cup of Coffee with My Interrogator*. I would write about 'Tea with the Tormentor'.

Javier interrupted only after he had rehearsed the sound of his voice. 'You have to understand that these things happened some time ago. The country no longer wants this debate, we have to move on to other things. . . .'

Snap . . . Lucho had pulled the hammer again and was studying the bullet.

'All I asked was "Did you like your job?" Did you enjoy doing what you did to those people you took prisoner?'

The question I had wanted to ask for more than twelve years had finally come out. Its origin lay not in an intellectual inquiry, but in a conversation in the early 1970s. The subject then had been the bonds and barriers in the mind, beyond pain, between torturer and victim. A dozen years ago we had been chatting in a suite at the Alvear Palace Hotel, Buenos Aires. Joan Baez, the singer, Joseph Novitsky, of the *Washington Post*, Jonathan Kandel of the *New York Times*, my wife and myself. Joan ate a steak, famished after a concert at the Luna Park. What was the condition in which men and women inflicted almost insufferable cruelty and then could communicate with the sufferer? Later the account of a woman in prison in Uruguay had been published. She had found one of her gaolers to be kind, caring, concerned about her circumstances. One day, during a ferocious session of torture with electricity, her anonymous tormentor had pulled the blind from her eyes for her to see the caring, kind gaoler smiling at her through clenched teeth.

My search was not for monsters but for names. My assumption was that torturers knew their victims and perhaps would help to determine their whereabouts. In my memory I had an album full of photographs of young people who had been taken from their homes at three o'clock in the morning. Fresh faces of men and women, some posing for an engagement picture, young mothers and fathers with babies, girls with grannies, boys with dads.... The last vision was of Alejandra Jaimovich, a sweet face with a nervous smile at a graduation ceremony in Córdoba. She was abducted at the age of eighteen as a member of a group called the *Guevarist Youth*, which by then she had long left. She was not considered a threat then: but military evaluation said she would be a security risk in six years' time.

I took out a letter. 'Let me read you this: "the programme went out on the 14th and 24th of April 1982. It consisted of questions put to five people the journalist had gathered and who had problems with some of the disappeared. Each stated their experience. One said he had left Argentina several months after the military coup of '76, with his whole family. He said he had worked as a motorcar or motorcycle mechanic for the Police and he had seen *things*. When he was asked what he had seen, he said he would tell but only if his name was erased from the tape. This was agreed and he said: 'I have seen how young people were sat down, their feet were placed in two receptacles and Portland cement poured in; when it hardened a little they were picked up and taken away. As for what they did to the young women, that I cannot tell out of respect for the ladies who are present.... I am sending you a list of the *desaparecidos* we have here. Much love to you both."'

Snap

'Lucho, put that gun away,' I shouted.

'Ha, ha, I've got you. You're shit scared. Brave journalists are shit scared. Think what a good headline that could make in *La Razon*. Or in *Cronica*: "*English pirate shit-scared journalist...*"

'So you want to know what we did, eh? He wants to know, Javier... OK, I'll tell you... Where did that letter come from, eh?'

'Israel,' I replied.

'Jewish sons of bitches ... you can't trust them. Can I see the letter?'

'No.'

'Stuff it. I don't really want it. If I did I would have it off you like this.' He swung the gun and I almost handed over the piece of paper. Our host stood up and preached calm. He said we were all interested in history and what Lucho and Javier could tell was useful because it was 'live history'.

'I'll tell you. You can do nothing to me because you don't know who I am and our friend won't tell you. Besides, I'm not ashamed of what I did. . . .'

'So you did enjoy your work,' I remarked, and realised how foolish it sounded.

'Christ, that's the third time you say that. You sound like a pervert. We did a job, at least I did. In the army we were in Córdoba; we had our orders and that was that. Our mission was to get the ERP (People's Revolutionary Army – a Marxist group), and trade union subversives. The navy worked on the Montoneros, the Air Force on the Trotskyists and the Workers Power communist group. Naturally, borders were crossed, but those were the original targets. We operated in cells. There is no other way to beat the communists.

'If we had lost, who would speak for us? Just a few mad Croatian and Polish exiles. Nobody else would care; even if we were decapitated and our heads put on spikes in Plaza de Mayo. The propaganda would have said it was in the cause of revolution.'

I said that I thought Polish dissidents in Poland were treated as VIPs compared with Argentine rebels.

'That is because the Pole rebels are merely an irritation; a nuisance to society. Here there was a threat to a way of life, to the church and the system. Anyway, the communists killed millions, and only the exiled East Europeans bother to remind us.'

Was there no thought in his mind for the people who had suffered the cruelty? I asked.

'It was not cruelty, it was a war.'

Was there no concern for individual rights when every legal clause was by-passed? I insisted.

'Don't give me that nonsense about human rights. That is just a political slogan. We were the real defenders of rights. We fought for a way of life, for a society without subversives. The rest is *mierda*. Those people who organise campaigns and wave flags do so either because they are militants or because it's safe. I agree with the people who say that the relatives, each and everyone, have to be told what happened to their subversive kin; but privately, eh! With no public scandal. Either that or shoot them all, so that there can be no campaigns. I don't give a damn. The command does though. The command is worried about policy and image. The higher you go the less you want to be involved with personal issues – policies, yes, but not persons.'

Javier remained silent. His apprehension at the course of the conversation seemed to have subsided, and he was pleased to let Lucho discuss politics.

What became unpleasant about the conversation was not the interlocutors, but its reasonableness. The discussion contained the almost casual contrasts of horror and normality of an extract from the Journal of Ernst Jünger, the German governor of Paris during the Second World War. For a long time, they had thought they had committed the perfect crime. There were no bodies and there was full support from the authorities. Events could be discussed without the violence of accusation and defence.

'That letter you read just now ... I can't say if it happened or not; so many things happened, many tough things. I don't think I could relive all that I did, even if I have no regrets. As Javier told you, there is a limit to how much you can take. The younger men seemed to be much much harsher. They were given authority over the subversives, and they made it a power over life and death.'

'How old were they?' I asked.

'Very young. Conscription age boys who had signed on as regulars, young corporals.... They had to be stopped from giving punishment, because they would have left the investigators with nobody to question. If anybody tells me that the young are idealistic ... after what I have seen... The young are all extremists – in their ideals, their violence, their moods. They don't know caution or care.'

He turned the pistol over in his hands, squinted down the sight, glanced through the window and aimed at a point. The building had become silent. The sound of lifts and steps and doors slamming had stopped as offices had emptied at the end of the day.

'We often had to restrain the very young,' Javier whined. He sounded like a schoolboy aspiring to be prefect.

'Did you ever use the "machine"? Did you ever have people on the grill?' I asked Javier. He stuttered, gasping for the right word.

'Of course he did,' Lucho broke in with a sneer. 'We all did... We all had to learn to give punishments to the subversives. It was a job. Can't you understand that...?'

Snap.

The secret was not to annoy Lucho. He began to play with the gun as soon as he lost his patience. The hammer must have been about to perforate the detonator and render the bullet useless, which was the object of the game. Or it would go off, and he would lose the game.

'Who were the ...?' I was about to say victims and remembered that he said subversives. But he understood the question.

'Mostly, we did not know. Sometimes we knew, if they were brought to us more than once. Usually, they were no more than a cypher. The men who had to pick them up knew the names, but they just delivered. You were either on pick-up or on punishment, not both. If you were on pick-up, you not only had to deliver, but also report on the operation and list the goods seized for inspection....'

Loot?

'No, not loot: confiscation. They had no more use for it. It was processed. The clothes went to orphanages of charities. Furniture was given away or sold. Cash went to a special fund....'

'For looters?'

'As bonus payments for the members for the Task Group; to arrange operations which could not be completed without money.'

Who handled the money? I asked.

'Agents, brokers, property dealers – there are always people available to handle any kind of money without questions as long as it is enough.'

My next question was whether Lucho could describe a day's routine.

'There was none. If we were on operations, it was night work; and we were on call. If we were at base, on punishment, we were called in whenever a new batch arrived. You had to go to work immediately; no questions, no time wasting. Their clothes were torn off, they were pushed onto a metal table, strapped down and they got the electricity.'

Javier was pouring sweat. 'I didn't do that for long, I asked to be moved to operations – and from there I left.' Lucho smiled at him: 'the youngest were the regulars on the Machine. It was enough to tell them, "That is your enemy, a communist" and for them it was just like a football match. They had to beat the other side.'

I asked about a report in the newspaper *Pueblo*, in Madrid, which had interviewed a young woman recently. She had reappeared after three years in captivity. She was quoted as saying: 'At times they tortured several people at the same time. They even placed bets to see who endured greater torture.'

'That would be the young ones. We had several of those in Córdoba.'

Where?

'In Córdoba.'

But where?

'In Córdoba. It must have been the young ones. The older ones who hung on in that business were sick. Our lot, those in the middle, were moved from one place to another so that we would not get ill.'

How did 'they' feel? It was not easy for me to give 'them' a name.

'I thought you wanted to talk about "us", not them.'

The navy man, our host, was smiling. What was he laughing at. 'The way you two are carrying on. It is like a game of ping pong.'

We had reached a point where the questions had to continue. When had Lucho tortured people?

'I never tortured. Torture is inflicting pain for personal pleasure. I dealt punishment to my enemy, under orders from my superiors. And if you want to know, we all get to the stage when it becomes a game: the subversive knows that. You are playing to get things out of him. Time is on your side, but you cannot give him time, because then he will gain on you as you begin to realise what you are doing. I am working to break him as quickly as possible. You feel sorry to cause pain, but you work quickly. You don't look at the face, even when you put the prods in the mouth; you keep their eyes covered. The secret is not to look at their eyes. The other secret is do not draw blood, leave that for the sick bastards or the young brutes. You can watch the body arch and bounce under electricity but never draw blood....'

What voltage was used?

'Anything up to 220 volts. Then they got the submarine, they were hung from the feet and dipped into a pool of dirty water or dropped on a damp floor covered with coarse salt.... But I never did that. Electricity is clean. The rest is for the maniacs.'

There were spots in front of my eyes as the blood drained from my face. Lucho was sweating, too, and the autumn chill in the office was unnoticed.

'The Montoneros said we took *falopa* (drugs). But we did not need it. We were doing our duty as officers. They used drugs; we often caught them so full of drugs that they could not hold a gun on anybody.'

His growing desperation gave me strength.

Did anybody ever die on him?

'Never. But two froze on Javier,' he grinned cruelly at the other man. Lucho knew that this would cause discomfort. So that was why Javier had cracked; but had it happened by accident or zeal? Javier was not answering. Our host was very stiff, and nervous.

Lucho continued: 'You couldn't help but get excited, when you were handling a naked body, totally at your mercy. The movement became demanding, their semi-conscious vulnerability a temptation. You had to do it...'

Lucho quoted Flaubert, 'A man has missed something if he has never woken up in an anonymous bed beside a face he'll never see again, and if he never left a brothel at dawn feeling like jumping off a bridge out of sheer physical disgust with life.'

'You feel terrible,' he chuckled softly – 'It's like a hangover, and putrid bile is in your throat and nostrils. But you do it. And then life goes on. You live or you kill yourself.'

Our host was pale. He seemed about to break down. 'You bastard. I had never allowed myself to believe these terrible stories.'

Lucho looked down at his lap.

Snap.

'For Christ sake put that gun down, will you!'

Lucho, his eyes to the floor, lifted the pistol and half threw it on the desk. The sound of thunder-clap filled the room. The marked bullet in the chamber had exploded. Javier's tea cup, standing on the end of the desk and opposite Lucho, vanished in what seemed to be a cloud of white dust. It ceased to exist other than in powdered form.

All four of us stood and stared at the hole in the wall, level with the desk.

Through a piercing whine sound in my ears, I heard a little croaking noise from our host. At last he found enough voice to say 'It would be better if you all left.'

I was out of the office and on *Avenida* Corrientes without being conscious of the descent by the stairs. My feet took me home along Florida Street, guided by a sense of direction rather than by sight – bumping into people, plant pots and litter bins, in the manner of one recently blinded.

13

POSTSCRIPT TO CHAPTER THREE

November 1984

If Mario Eduardo Firmenich, commander of Argentina's Montoneros guerrillas, is sent down for a long stretch, and if I some day get a bullet between the eyes, the source of both events will have to be sought in a short chapter, the third in this book.

In 1981 Junction Books, London, published a smaller version of the book, entitled *Portrait of an Exile*. Although it was not officially banned, it didn't circulate in Argentina. Its contents were matters that people whispered about, but did not like to be seen reading. However, later in February 1984, a weekly news magazine in Buenos Aires, *Somos*, translated and published Chapter Three and said I was a key witness to the release of Jorge Born. Mario Eduardo Firmenich had recently been arrested in Brazil. Two months earlier, the new constitutional government in Argentina had issued two decrees which ordered the arrest and trial of the military officers and the guerrilla leaders who had plunged Argentina into a 'dry war' for the previous ten years.

The Argentine government asked Brazil for the extradition of Firmenich. France and Greece offered to grant Firmenich asylum. It was a generous offer to the government: they were giving Argentina a chance to relieve itself of the problem of putting Firmenich on trial.

Extradition seemed unlikely. There was a strong lobby in Brazil to secure the release of Firmenich, still considered a revolutionary.

Why had he surrendered? Under whose protection was he, when he had gone to the Argentine Consulate to renew his papers, and why was he only arrested on his fourth call? Whose assurance of safety did he have? Whose caution was disregarded? Or was he seeking protection through arrest? He had been advocating a more peaceful role for the Montoneros. The Argentine State Security Secretariat (SIDE) had spread the rumour that Firmenich had rejected a plan to break out of Brazilian arrest, in fear of being done in by his own men. I was asked to go to Buenos Aires to testify in court. The invitation seemed irrelevant. Firmenich's extradition was only a remote possibility.

Extradition, however, was granted in September. Firmenich was flown to Buenos Aires in October. I was flown to Argentina, a witness for the prosecution, on 17 November.

I had been trusted by the guerrillas at one time. Yet the organization had once ordered a bomb to be planted in my desk; the man who had taken this decision had told me so himself. It was because of an article in the *Buenos Aires Herald*.

Firmenich's politics were violent, his methods neo-Fascist. And from the comfort of exile in Cuba he had ordered his followers, also exiles, some of them very young and innocent, back into combat in Argentina and to ignominious and horrifying death by the bloodied military, who lusted for such slaughter. Yet Firmenich was no more than a product of his time, and as such he had acted.

In going back to his trial, I was only trying to prove to myself that I had the time and inclination to support the only system of government – a constitutional one – that I think I want for Argentina, the country where I was born and which I still love. I was also travelling on an ego trip: I wanted to say that Chapter Three was the truth.

To encourage my journey to Buenos Aires, the Argentine Government had offered protection.

The Spanish Security agent came into the London newsroom on the Friday afternoon (16 November, 1984). He asked if I was ready. I had my ticket, and was leaving for Argentina on

Saturday. He wanted to leave right away. I had a party I was not going to miss ... There is all of immortality in which to be teetotal.

He showed no guns, but his voice had the clipped manner of command. If this was security, it seemed quite unnecessary. He looked uncomfortable, exposed. He had orders: 'We are from Spanish government security, and we have orders to take you to Madrid. It would be helpful if you helped me to obey.'

Somebody called 'This way,' grabbed my arm and guided me through the side door in the pier, down the metal steps to the Madrid tarmac. All the guns that had not been seen in London came out now, in belts, in shoulder holsters, in hands. The man who had called out introduced himself. He said that his colleagues had orders to take care of me. It was a request from the Argentine government and they were going to comply.

One car took me to the perimeter of the airport; another car which waited with three men inside surrounded by Guardia Civil, took me into a Madrid I was not allowed to see. There had been threats, they said. I was their guest while I was in Madrid. They would drive me to the airport later for the Argentine Airlines flight to Buenos Aires. The safe house was across the street from the French ambassador's residence: a large apartment on the third floor of an elegant building. There we had to wait for the Argentine pick-up. The appointment was at 6pm.

The Argentine security agent repeatedly said that he was there to protect me, and assured that he was not playing games. It was a prelude to the opening of a case full of make-up, hairdressing accessories, wigs, lotions. When I refused to shave off my beard, it was dyed an aged grey, almost white; and my hair was changed to black. A few hours later I would discover that the dye on my beard was temporary: it crackled and looked like dandruff when it dropped on my tie. The dye on my hair was permanent. I was also given a pair of glasses. The Spanish officers were delighted. They promised me great success with young women.

Then I was taken out to supper; again the mystery was manic. Three men were with me, chattering about security, Gibraltar, the EEC; two sat at the table next to ours; guns were under newspapers, on chairs, in belts; eyes roamed the premises. Finally, they drove through all the airport security into the guts of the restricted-area, where I was handed over to a group of policemen. They were talking to two younger men about birth control. Strange how police hold conversations just like ordinary people.

They glanced at me and changed the subject. Two of their number had been killed by a terror group that seemed to have no line or ideology. The chief of the police, in plainclothes, remembered where he and the others had worked together, 'When we chased that gang in the Pyrenees and you broke a leg ... We were also together when we went after the gold people in Galicia.'

The plane was searched for bombs with explosive detectors. Police had taken over the airport, and every flight list was checked. As an ordinary mortal there should have been a sense of importance, of privilege, even excitement. But there was more a feeling of exhaustion, a desire to be elsewhere, without being afraid. I was only going back to revisit events of a decade ago. There was no apprehension, just sleepiness. Arthur Koestler wrote in *Dialogue with Death* that sleep was a gimmick of the subconscious to preserve the balance of the conscious.

The crew of Argentine Airlines Flight 153 had been told that they would be informed in Buenos Aires of the reason for the precautions, not before.

One stewardess asked about the special passenger and was severely reprimanded. One of the security agents immediately, furtively, comforted her. It was almost like the old game in every operation. There was always a bad guy who shouted threats and questions, and a good guy who offered helpful advice. One of the men told stewardesses a string of tales of international intrigue and daring operations in which he had been involved.

The in-flight movie was *Gorky Park*. I slept right through

it. Rio de Janeiro has an attractive airport from which no plane ever leaves on time. The Brazilian authorities ordered us to leave the plane in order to lose any shadowers. The order to change planes came from Brasilia, the capital: there was a rumour of a threat against my life. My guards were furious – two sympathetic blondes in First Class had to be left behind. A line of police officers and government officials greeted me on the tarmac in Buenos Aires. There were six cars with heavily-armed men. I was driven to the flat of a friend of mine, which they stormed, for security reasons, terrifying my host – who was then on the telephone to a girlfriend.

I was given a twenty-four-hour guard; three men at the door, one on the stairs, three on the ground floor; a car waited at all times to take me anywhere. I was in complete freedom, thoroughly controlled. The officer commanding the first shift introduced himself with a speech: 'We thank you for coming to help in the battle against subversion. I have fought the guerrillas for many years.'

'Were you a clean fighter, or one of those who tortured people and made them disappear?' I asked. He listened patiently and justified the use of terror with the teachings of the Bible. My abuse made me the man of violence: he, with all his guns, was the man of peace. Softly he remarked that in Europe there was legalized abortion, which was the murder of innocents. He was quite ready to admit to torture and killing people.

He was my age, and ten years before he perhaps was one of the officers who might have tried to kill me, when they were ordered to raid the newspaper where I worked. These people – at least, theirs was the same branch – were now making sure that I remained alive.

Friends came to the flat. The display of security and weapons was uncomfortable: long-barrelled FAL (light machine-guns), Ingram submachine pistols, Colt .45 pistols, 9mm, 38mm, dozens of rounds of ammunition, safety catches slipped on and off whenever people came and left, walkie-talkies crackling their metallic language at regular intervals ... Friends had to produce documents before they could enter; it was like living in fiction. The guards warned one woman that, if she was photographed in my company, either side could do her in and blame the other.

Next morning, Monday, was the first session in court, and of reliving the events of ten years before. The guards drove fast, but were mindful of road rules. Ten years ago, I had been in the same court, then on criminal charges for defying the military censors. Under the military despots, police did not stop at red traffic lights. Now at least they obeyed certain street niceties, as far as anybody does in Argentina.

There was a group of photographers at the court. I brushed by them. After a briefing by the prosecutor, we went to see the judge. Both had been threatened; they went around with an escort, not as big as mine, they assured me. We chatted before entering court. The prosecutor contorted his face in a sequence of grimaces directed at me. He was trying to tell me that my flies were open.

In court I was presented with an official translation of Chapter Three. An autographed copy was required by the judge, but it was promptly snatched from him by the clerk and slammed into a safe. The deposition said a copy would be kept in the court safe.

Several hours later I was driven home – I collapsed on the sofa, exhausted. My host mixed drinks, without questions. There were a few visitors, but most friends chose to stay away. A friend came and autographed a volume of her short stories. 'May we meet again in a time without fear.'

A right-wing anglophile telephoned to ask for my support to get George Canning out of the 46th Police Precinct.

'What...?'

Yes, he had been there since an anti-British demo had torn him off his pedestal under the English clock tower and had thrown him in the river.

On the second night I began to know my guards better. The officer who had been a torturer and killer was always on the telephone to his superiors to ask for more guns. One man read the Bible every night. He was a music teacher who demonstrated his proficiency on my guitar, which I had left behind years before, with a delightful concert of Aranjuez and some tango. He then remembered how he had picked pieces of Julio Sosa, the Uruguayan tango singer, out of a crashed car. The guitarist's pistol lay on the coffee table all the time while he played and talked.

One guard was monothematic: women.

Another was an old man on the night shift; he usually fell asleep in the small hours. He carried a sub-machinegun, and sat over it, looking so crumpled and with shoulders so hunched that his lapels curled forward to meet under his chin. Once I spied on him, unseen, as he leaned on his long barrel, a machine-pistol by his side. I could have taken it and shot him, and shot each man who came up in the lift or by the stairs. It would put the lift out for a week. I brushed away the thought with my hand. Again, I was the man of violence. The men of guns were at peace, asleep.

Tuesday brought the need to identify the house where the press conference had taken place. It had been found by court officials from the description in Chapter Three. The new owner had been offended by my derogatory observations about the design. But it seems that the house had already come under scrutiny for its use in a previous kidnapping. A young Jewish boy had been kidnapped and held there; he had been ransomed, but his captors had killed him. After the boy's death, the previous owner had fled abroad. That owner had worked with the Montoneros, but had been recruited for counter-espionage by one of the security services. He had used this as a cover and had entered into partnership with an officer to arrange the boy's kidnapping for profit. After his departure, the Montoneros had used the house for the press conference, for the release of Born, and perhaps also to hold him for some time before that.

The court clerk arrived first, with typewriter and paper to take my deposition. Then came the judge with his guards, the prosecutor with his guard, and I, the witness, with guards. The street was cut off, and filled with men in grey suits carrying pistols and machineguns. The owner offered coffee and mineral water and explained the occasion to his neighbours. The prosecutor advised him to sell and get out.

I went to lunch with my mates from newspaper days. I needed to know what they thought about what I was doing. It was a grand reunion. My colleagues of a generation ago did not shun me as a squealer. I was embraced and kissed, and they said they were pleased to see me. But they were glad the guards did not come up with me.

The guitar teacher had said that we should keep my instrument in a case; otherwise the wood might be damaged. So we went to buy a guitar case. Into a music shop we marched, three men as escort, two more in a car waiting in the street. He, too, probably thought of the guitar case in the Chicago gangster films. The guards looked for suspects behind the drums and the flutes. My guards wanted me to take a woman to the flat. 'You must think that you are here for a short time only. You have had a good steak, and good wine. But you also should think of a woman. We'll take you wherever you want, we'll wait outside the door, we'll cheer you on.' Whenever we passed a well-endowed woman on the street they would ask: 'Wouldn't you like her? Shall we stop and pick her up?' I wondered if they used their guns to gain such favours.

The *Buenos Aires Herald*, where I had spent ten years of my life, telephoned to ask for details of my story. I growled, intolerant with contemporaries who have forgotten the history they have lived, and impatient with the young that never read it. In Argentina, the younger people had been advised not to read; the older chose to forget. With the end of dictatorship, it is a country that is trying to reconstruct a history of which it has kept no records.

Next day, another friend, Roberto, came to the flat and stayed late. We talked about how he had been tortured by the police – the same people who had tried to kill me and had squeezed him to find me. I had escaped into exile in London. We looked down a dozen storeys to the street, then instinctively moved away from the balcony and chatted in an inner room, well away from the front door.

Then Thursday ... the day of confrontation with Mario Eduardo Firmenich. His lawyer had asked for the meeting. The judge had ordered it.

The street outside the court was closed off. There were two armoured vehicles in front of the court. There were 200 men armed with rifles and machine-guns, and nests on the roof. Court employees peered, policemen tried to get a look, but the lady from across the road who sat in apron and curlers on her kitchen stool on the pavement had the best view of all.

I was put in a side room. I fell asleep in a chair; the police officers were surprised that this should occur before such an event. They apologized for waking me. We chatted about the world's underpaid police forces. Then I fell asleep again.

Firmenich heard a recording of the 1975 press conference. The Montoneros had made the recording and transcribed it into a pamphlet. The court had come into possession of the pamphlet, perhaps from a police raid; the recording had been seized at a local newspaper which had boasted of its possession.

Firmenich denied that the recording was genuine: anybody could have made it from the pamphlet. He admitted the pamphlet was his political statement. He admitted that the press conference had been held, but denied that he had any knowledge of Born's presence in the house or that he had been seen with Born. Such an admission would have made him a direct accomplice in the abduction and in the murder of one of Born's aides.

Confrontations of this kind usually last only a few minutes. The judge wanted to see who went into a sweat first.

Firmenich's hand trembled a little. He said 'hello' in a casual, almost friendly, manner to all present. The prosecutor tried an obvious ruse: 'I don't have to introduce you, you've met.' Firmenich said 'No, never.' I said we had. Firmenich had read my stories and described them as fantasy. It was easy for me. In the end I would go home; Firmenich would go back to his cell.

But he was in control, far more so than his lawyer, or even the judge. The judge listened; the lawyer, a veteran court operator, expostulated occasionally in a threatening manner. He had been defence counsel to the trade union headquarters for many years. He was now being shunned by his profession for taking up Firmenich's defence; in a few years' time, with a change in the political atmosphere, he may achieve high regard among nationalists. For the time being, he could only look forward to a substantial wad of dollars – which are better at buying respect than any other social concept.

The lawyer was trying to argue that the prosecution was politically motivated. If he could prove this, Firmenich would go free. The terms of the extradition from Brazil forbade trial on political issues. Only criminal charges could be considered valid.

The prosecutor had no other case as solid as this one. Firmenich was accused of masterminding two murders committed by Montoneros. But he had countered that he was then in Cuba and could not be held responsible for every action by his followers. The other action to which he had readily confessed – by means of a report in his organization's magazine – was participation in the kidnapping and murder of a former President. That was covered by the 1973 amnesty and therefore was untouchable. The Born case was the only big one for the prosecution and for the civilian government, which had to show the public that it was acting evenly against both the military murderers of the dictatorship and the guerrillas. Firmenich denied ever being with Born. He said I was mistaken. He was very polite, just as when he had said that we had never met. Of course we had, even as far back as 1974, on 'Journalist's Day' in a ramshackle old mansion in the Belgrano district, where he and Dardo Cabo (a noble nationalist, veteran activist, later murdered by the police in a sham escape attempt) and four or five journalists had argued for many hours over politics, ideology, armed action, and tactical operations. We were kept going that day by an unlimited supply of *empanadas* (pasties) and several large bottles of Coca Cola, served by two girls and an elderly woman (referred to as 'La Tia'), all of whom retreated into the kitchen. We had joked that the imperialism of the multinationals was present everywhere. That was history. Remember?

Firmenich asked, 'Could you not have seen Born come into the room after I had left? My officers organized the press con-

175

ference, but I was not to know who was in the house. This was as much for my organization's security as for my own.'

Firmenich looked carefully groomed, his hair neatly combed back and kept in place with setting cream, he looked healthy ... He looked like a million dollars – or was it sixty million? He was guilty of being the child of a generation in crisis. But that upheaval had caused the deaths of hundreds of young, some very young, men and women. He and the like-minded sadists in the army he had fought for power had pushed so many to horrible, lonely, lost deaths. It was a rich man's kidnapping that had brought Firmenich to court, but in my mind he was on trial for mass murder and for indirectly causing the military terror, which forced amnesia on a generation. He may not have been totally to blame for that: Argentina has never had the capacity to recollect that it loses some of its life every time it loses its memory. However, that is a paraphrase of Buñuel.

Firmenich had been in his early twenties when the Montoneros guerrillas were formed, Roman Catholic right-wing nationalists who fancied a left turn on the path to revolution ... Twelve characters in search of a script ... Their theatre was built in the graveyards.

His questions hinged on how many minutes before the press conference had I arrived? How many minutes after had I left? At what point had I seen him shake hands with Born? How long had the press conference lasted? I replied slowly, sure of my answers. He had been there with Born, and he was not going to get out of that accusation by wearing me down. The judge wanted to put an end to the meeting. Firmenich turned to him with voice firm and reasoning: 'Just a minute. We are talking about fifteen years of my life; give me the right to defend myself,' which shut up the judge and the prosecutor. To be sure that I was sure of myself, I told him that I was prepared to answer questions for as long as he wanted to ask them. His lawyer tried to rattle me; he used noise to gain advantage. He asked me about an article about me in a local magazine, which had translated some of Chapter Three. I said I knew nothing about it: 'You shouldn't trust journalists for your evidence.'

Firmenich smoked, offered cigarettes, cracked little political jokes. The lawyer made jokes too – about appointments of judges. He was probably trying to befriend the judge. He asked me for a copy of my book; but he could not read English.

After more than two hours, the judge said that the cross-examination by the defence had produced only minor changes in the testimony, and he ended the confrontation.

It was 10.30 pm when I was taken home. The guards had been waiting for hours for permission to change shift. The speed at which they drove home verged on road lunacy. The drivers weaved through the traffic, only occasionally using the sirens, more often terrifying other drivers as they slipped through the narrowest spaces and sped on. They spent long boring days on guard and this seemed their release. They had to get home too: their wages were low and most had one, or even two, more jobs elsewhere.

At the flat, my host and I chatted softly until the special watery pink of dawn over Buenos Aires coloured the sky. I started to pack for the flight to London.

Firmenich could be sentenced to twenty-five years on my testimony; though it seems more reasonable that an initial sentence could be for fifteen years and then depend on appeal. He cannot get life under the terms of extradition from Brazil. But he could be out in five years, which is what is left of this constitutional government's term. The incoming administration may be politically bound to dictate an amnesty for all, both military and civilian, who took part in the 'dirty war' of the 'seventies.

BIBLIOGRAPHY

Amnesty International: *Report of an Amnesty International Mission to Argentina*. London, March 1977.

Amnesty International: *The Disappeared of Argentina*. London, May 1979.

Amnesty International: *Testimony on Secret Detention Camps in Argentina*. London, 1979.

Argentina y sus derechos humanos (Asociación Patriótica Argentina), Buenos Aires, 1980.

Astrada, Etelvina (Editor): *Poesía política y combativa argentina*. Zero, Madrid, 1978.

Bonasso, Miguel: *Recuerdo de la muerte*. Brughera, Buenos Aires, 1984.

Bousquet, Jean-Pierre: *Les folles de la place de Mai*. Stock 2, Paris 1982.

Catholic Institute for International Relations: *Death and Violence in Argentina*. London, October 1976. (A report on attacks against the Roman Catholic Church and priests in Argentina.)

Chambenoix, Christian: Buenos Aires, the devouring capital. *Le Monde*. Paris, 17 May 1978.

Comisión Argentina por los Derechos Humanos: *Argentina: proceso al genocidio*. Elías Querejeta, Madrid, 1977.

Cox, Robert J: *The Sound of one hand clapping. A preliminary study of the Argentine press in a time of terror*. Woodrow Wilson International Centre, Washington DC, August, 1980.

Crawley, Eduardo: *Argentina, a house divided, 1880–1980*. Hurst, London 1984.

Cunninghame Graham, Robert B.: *Tales of Horsemen*. Canongate, Edinburgh, 1981.

Di Tella, Guido: *Argentina under Perón, 1973–1976*. St Anthony's/ Macmillan Series, London, 1981.

Ferrer, Aldo: *Living within our means: an examination of the Argentine economic crisis.* Third World Foundation for Social and Economic Studies, London, 1985.

Galeano, Eduardo: *Days and nights of love and war.* Monthly Review Press, New York, 1983.

Gillespie, Richard: *Soldiers of Perón: Argentina's Montonaros.* Oxford, 1982.

Giussani, Pablo: *La soberbia armada.* Sudamericana-Planeta, Buenos Aires, 1984.

Gòdio, Julio: La guerra imaginaria ha terminado. *Controversia.* Mexico, September 1980.

Graham-Yooll, Andrew: *The Press in Argentina, 1973–1978.* Writers and Scholars Educational Trust, London, 1979.

Graham-Yooll, Andrew: *The Forgotten colony, a history of the English-speaking communities in Argentina.* Hutchinson, London, 1981.

Graham-Yooll, Andrew: *Portrait of an exile.* Junction Books, London, 1981.

Graham-Yooll, Andrew: *Small wars you may have missed.* Junction Books, London, 1983.

Hodges, Donald C.: *Argentina, 1943–1976.* University of New Mexico Press, 1976.

Hoeffel, Paul: Missing or dead in Argentina. *The New York Times Magazine.* 21 May 1979.

Hudson, W. H: *Far away and long ago.* Eland Books, London,1982.

Johnson, Paul: The seven deadly sins of terrorism. *New Republic.* 1979 (Washington, 1980) (rep. *Dialogue.*)

Informe sobre los Derechos Humanos en la Argentina. Organización de los Estados Americanos, Washington, 1979.

Kahn, Heriberto: *Doy Fe.* Losada, Buenos Aires, 1979.

Lanusse, Alejandro: *Mi Testimonio.* Laserre Editores, Buenos Aires, 1977.

Main, Mary: *Evita, the woman with the whip.* Corgi, London, 1980.

Naipaul, V. S: *The return of Eva Perón.* André Deutsch, London, 1980.

Navarro, Marysa, and Fraser, Nicholas: *Eva Perón.* André Deutsch, London, 1980.

Neilson, James: *La vorágine argentina.* Marymar, Buenos Aires 1979. (53 pieces originally published in English by the *Buenos Aires Herald* between December 1972 and April 1976.)

Page, Joseph: *Perón, a biography*. Random House, New York, 1983.

Rouquié, Alain: *Poder militar y sociedad política en la Argentina*. (2 vols.) Emece, Buenos Aires, 1982.

Sábato, Ernesto: *Apologías y rechazos*. Seix Barral, Barcelona, 1979.

Sábato, Ernesto, and Argentine National Commission on Disappeared People: *Nunca Más (Never again)*. Faber/Index on Censorship, London, 1986.

Soriano, Osvaldo: *No habrá más penas ni olvido*. Bruguera, Barcelona, 1980.

Taylor, J. M.: *Evita Perón, the Myths of a Woman*. Blackwell, Oxford, 1979.

Terragno, Rodolfo: *Contratapas*. Ediciones Cuestionario, Buenos Aires, May 1976.

Terragno, Rodolfo: *La Argentina del Siglo 21*. Sudamericana-Planeta, 1985.

Theroux, Paul: *The old Patagonian express*. Hamish Hamilton, London, 1979.

Timerman, Jacobo: *Prisoner without a name, cell without a number*. Weidenfeld and Nicolson, London, 1981.

Vacca, Roberto, and Borroni, Otelo: *La vida de Eva Perón*. Vol. 1. Galerna, Buenos Aires, 1970.

Vazquez, María Esther: *Borges: imágenes, memorias, diálogos*. Monte Avila, Caracas, 1977.

Walsh, María Elena: Desventuras en el país-jardín-de-infantes. *Clarín*. Buenos Aires, 16 August 1979.

West, Morris: *Proteus*. Collins, London, 1979.

MEMOIRS OF A
BENGAL CIVILIAN

JOHN BEAMES
**The lively narrative of a Victorian
district-officer**

With an introduction by Philip Mason

They are as entertaining as Hickey . . . accounts like
these illuminate the dark corners of history.
Times Literary Supplement

John Beames writes a splendidly virile English and
he is incapable of being dull; also he never hesitates
to speak his mind. It is extraordinary that these
memoirs should have remained so long unpublished
. . . the discovery is a real find.
John Morris, The Listener

A gem of the first water. Beames, in addition to being
a first-class descriptive writer in the plain Defoesque
manner, was that thing most necessary of all in an
autobiographer – an original. His book is of the
highest value.
The Times

*If you wish to receive details of forthcoming publications,
please send your address to
Eland Books, 53 Eland Road, London SW11 5JX*

Previously published by
ELAND BOOKS

A VISIT TO DON OTAVIO

SYBILLE BEDFORD
A Mexican Journey

I am convinced that, once this wonderful book becomes better known, it will seem incredible that it could ever have gone out of print.
Bruce Chatwin, Vogue

This book can be recommended as vastly enjoyable. Here is a book radiant with comedy and colour.
Raymond Mortimer, Sunday Times

Perceptive, lively, aware of the significance of trifles, and a fine writer. Applied to a beautiful, various, and still inscrutable country, these talents yield a singularly delightful result.
The Times

This book has that ageless quality which is what most people mean when they describe a book as classical. From the moment that the train leaves New York. . .it is certain that this journey will be rewarding. When one finally leaves Mrs Bedford on the point of departure, it is with the double regret of leaving Mexico and her company, and one cannot say more than that.
Elizabeth Jane Howard

Malicious, friendly, entertaining and witty.
Evening Standard

This edition is not for sale in the USA

*If you wish to receive details of forthcoming publications,
please send your address to
Eland Books, 53 Eland Road, London SW11 5JX*

VIVA MEXICO!

CHARLES MACOMB FLANDRAU
A traveller's account of life in Mexico

With a new preface by Nicholas Shakespeare

His lightness of touch is deceiving, for one reads *Viva Mexico!* under the impression that one is only being amused, but comes to realise in the end that Mr Flandrau has presented a truer, more graphic and comprehensive picture of the Mexican character than could be obtained from a shelful of more serious and scientific tomes.
New York Times

The best book I have come upon which attempts the alluring but difficult task of introducing the tricks and manners of one country to the people of another.
Alexander Woollcott

Probably the best travel book I have ever read.
Miles Kington, Times

His impressions are deep, sympathetic and judicious. In addition, he is a marvellous writer, with something of Mark Twain's high spirits and Henry James's suavity ... as witty as he is observant.
Geoffrey Smith, Country Life

*If you wish to receive details of forthcoming publications,
please send your address to
Eland Books, 53 Eland Road, London SW11 5JX*

Previously published by
ELAND BOOKS

TRAVELS WITH MYSELF AND ANOTHER

MARTHA GELLHORN

Must surely be ranked as one of the funniest travel books of our time — second only to *A Short Walk in the Hindu Kush* . . . It doesn't matter whether this author is experiencing marrow-freezing misadventures in war-ravaged China, or driving a Landrover through East African game-parks, or conversing with hippies in Israel, or spending a week in a Moscow Intourist Hotel. Martha Gellhorn's reactions are what count and one enjoys equally her blistering scorn of humbug, her hilarious eccentricities, her unsentimental compassion.
Dervla Murphy, Irish Times

Spun with a fine blend of irony and epigram. She is incapable of writing a dull sentence.
The Times

Miss Gellhorn has a novelist's eye, a flair for black comedy and a short fuse . . . there is not a boring word in her humane and often funny book.
The New York Times

Among the funniest and best written books I have ever read.
Byron Rogers, Evening Standard

*If you wish to receive details of forthcoming publications,
please send your address to
Eland Books, 53 Eland Road, London SW11 5JX*

Previously published by
ELAND BOOKS

THE
WEATHER
IN
AFRICA

MARTHA GELLHORN

This is a stunningly good book.
Victoria Glendinning, New York Times

She's a marvellous story-teller, and I think anyone who picks up this book is certainly not going to put it down again. One just wants to go on reading.
Francis King, Kaleidoscope, BBC Radio 4

An authentic sense of the divorce between Africa and what Europeans carry in their heads is powerfully conveyed by a prose that selects its details with care, yet remains cool in their expression.
Robert Nye, The Guardian

This is a pungent and witty book.
Jeremy Brooks, Sunday Times

If you wish to receive details of forthcoming publications,
please send your address to
Eland Books, 53 Eland Road, London SW11 5JX

Previously published by
ELAND BOOKS

MOROCCO THAT WAS

WALTER HARRIS

With a new preface by Patrick Thursfield

Both moving and hilariously satirical.
Gavin Maxwell, Lords of the Atlas

Many interesting sidelights on the customs and characters of the Moors. . .intimate knowledge of the courts, its language and customs. . .thorough understanding of the Moorish character.
New York Times

No Englishman knows Morocco better than Mr W. B. Harris and his new book. . .is most entertaining.
Spectator (1921)

The author's great love of Morocco and of the Moors is only matched by his infectious zest for life. . . thanks to his observant eye and a gift for felicitously turned phrases, the books of Walter Harris can claim to rank as literature.
Rom Landau, Moroccan Journal (1957)

His pages bring back the vanished days of the unfettered Sultanate in all their dark splendour; a mingling of magnificence with squalor, culture with barbarism, refined cruelty with naive humour that reads like a dream of the Arabian Nights.
The Times

If you wish to receive details of forthcoming publications, please send your address to Eland Books, 53 Eland Road, London SW11 5JX

Previously published by
ELAND BOOKS

FAR AWAY
AND LONG AGO

W. H. HUDSON
A Childhood in Argentina

With a new preface by Nicholas Shakespeare

One cannot tell how this fellow gets his effects; he writes as the grass grows.
It is as if some very fine and gentle spirit were whispering to him the sentences he puts down on the paper. A privileged being
Joseph Conrad

Hudson's work is a vision of natural beauty and of human life as it might be, quickened and sweetened by the sun and the wind and the rain, and by fellowship with all other forms of life. . .a very great writer. . .the most valuable our age has possessed.
John Galsworthy

And there was no one – no writer – who did not acknowledge without question that this composed giant was the greatest living writer of English.
Far Away and Long Ago is the most self-revelatory of all his books.
Ford Madox Ford

Completely riveting and should be read by everyone.
Auberon Waugh

If you wish to receive details of forthcoming publications,
please send your address to
Eland Books, 53 Eland Road, London SW11 5JX

Previously published by
ELAND BOOKS

THREE CAME HOME

AGNES KEITH
A woman's ordeal in a Japanese prison camp

Three Came Home should rank with the great imprisonment
stories of all times.
New York Herald Tribune

No one who reads her unforgettable narrative of the years she
passed in Borneo during the war years can fail to share her
emotions with something very like the intensity of a personal
experience.
Times Literary Supplement

This book sets a standard which will be difficult to surpass.
The Listener

It is one of the most remarkable books you will ever read.
John Carey, Sunday Times

*If you wish to receive details of forthcoming publications,
please send your address to
Eland Books, 53 Eland Road, London SW11 5JX*

Previously published by
ELAND BOOKS

A DRAGON APPARENT

NORMAN LEWIS
Travels in Cambodia, Laos and Vietnam

A book which should take its place in the permanent literature of the Far East.
Economist

One of the most absorbing travel books I have read for a very long time. . .the great charm of the work is its literary vividness. Nothing he describes is dull.
Peter Quennell, Daily Mail

One of the best post-war travel books and, in retrospect, the most heartrending.
The Observer

Apart from *The Quiet American*, which is of course a novel, the best book on Vietnam remains *A Dragon Apparent*.
Richard West, Spectator (1978)

One of the most elegant, witty, immensely readable, touching and tragic books I've ever read.
Edward Blishen, Radio 4

If you wish to receive details of forthcoming publications, please send your address to
Eland Books, 53 Eland Road, London SW11 5JX

GOLDEN EARTH

NORMAN LEWIS
Travels in Burma

Mr Lewis can make even a lorry interesting.
Cyril Connolly, Sunday Times

Very funny . . . a really delightful book.
Maurice Collis, Observer

Norman Lewis remains the best travel writer alive.
Auberon Waugh, Business Traveller

The reader may find enormous pleasure here without knowing the country.
Honor Tracy, New Statesman

The brilliance of the Burmese scene is paralleled by the brilliance of the prose.
Guy Ramsey, Daily Telegraph

If you wish to receive details of forthcoming publications,
please send your address to
Eland Books, 53 Eland Road, London SW11 5JX

NAPLES '44

NORMAN LEWIS

As unique an experience for the reader as it must
have been a unique experience for the writer.
Graham Greene

Uncommonly well written, entertaining despite its
depressing content, and quite remarkably evocative.
Philip Toynbee, Observer

His ten novels and five non-fiction works place him
in the front rank of contemporary English writers . . .
here is a book of gripping fascination in its flow of
bizarre anecdote and character sketch; and it is
much more than that.
J. W. Lambert, Sunday Times

A wonderful book.
Richard West, Spectator

Sensitive, ironic and intelligent.
Paul Fussell, The New Republic

One goes on reading page after page as if eating
cherries.
Luigi Barzini, New York Review of Books

If you wish to receive details of forthcoming publications,
please send your address to
Eland Books, 53 Eland Road, London SW11 5JX

Previously published by
ELAND BOOKS

A VIEW
OF THE WORLD

NORMAN LEWIS
Selected Journalism

Here is the selected journalism of Norman Lewis,
collected from a period of over thirty years. The
selection includes ten of the best articles from *The
Changing Sky*, eight more which have never been
collected within a book, and two which have
never previously been published.

From reviews of *The Changing Sky*:

He really goes in deep like a sharp polished
knife. I have never travelled in my armchair so
fast, variously and well.
V. S. Pritchett, New Statesman

He has compressed into these always
entertaining and sophisticated sketches material
that a duller man would have hoarded for half a
dozen books.
The Times

Outstandingly the best travel writer of our age, if
not the best since Marco Polo.
Auberon Waugh, Business Traveller

*If you wish to receive details of forthcoming publications,
please send your address to
Eland Books, 53 Eland Road, London SW11 5JX*

A YEAR IN MARRAKESH

PETER MAYNE

A notable book, for the author is exceptional both in his literary talent and his outlook. His easy economical style seizes, with no sense of effort, the essence of people, situations and places . . . Mr Mayne is that rare thing, a natural writer . . . no less exceptional is his humour.
Few Westerners have written about Islam with so little nonsense and such understanding.
Times Literary Supplement.

He has contrived in a deceptively simple prose to disseminate in the air of an English November the spicy odours of North Africa; he has turned, for an hour, smog to shimmering sunlight. He has woven a texture of extraordinary charm.
Daily Telegraph

Mr Mayne's book gives us the 'strange elation' that good writing always creates. It is a good book, an interesting book, and one that I warmly recommend.
Harold Nicolson, Observer

If you wish to receive details of forthcoming publications,
please send your address to
Eland Books, 53 Eland Road, London SW11 5JX

Previously published by
ELAND BOOKS

KENYA DIARY (1902–1906)

RICHARD MEINERTZHAGEN

With a new preface by Elspeth Huxley

Those who have only read the tranquil descriptions of Kenya between the two Wars may be surprised by Meinertzhagen's often bloodthirsty diaries. They do not always make pleasant reading, but they offer an unrivalled and startlingly vivid account of life during the early days of the colony.

One of the best and most colourful intelligence officers the army ever had.
Times, Obituary

This book is of great interest and should not be missed
New Statesman

One of the ablest and most successful brains I had met in the army.
Lloyd George, Memoirs

Anybody at all interested in the evolution of Kenya or the workings of 'colonialism' would do well to read this diary.
William Plomer, Listener

If you wish to receive details of forthcoming publications,
please send your address to
Eland Books, 53 Eland Road, London SW11 5JX

Previously published by

ELAND BOOKS

JOURNEYS OF A GERMAN IN ENGLAND

CARL PHILIP MORITZ
A walking-tour of England in 1782

With a new preface by Reginald Nettel

The extraordinary thing about the book is that the writing is so fresh that you are startled when a stage-coach appears. A young man is addressing himself to you across two centuries. And there is a lovely comedy underlying it.
Byron Rogers, Evening Standard

This account of his travels has a clarity and freshness quite unsurpassed by any contemporary descriptions.
Iain Hamilton, Illustrated London News

A most amusing book. . .a variety of small scenes which might come out of Hogarth. . .Moritz in London, dodging the rotten oranges flung about the pit of the Haymarket Theatre, Moritz in the pleasure gardens of Vauxhall and Ranelagh, Moritz in Parliament or roving the London streets is an excellent companion. We note, with sorrow, that nearly two centuries ago, British coffee was already appalling.
Alan Pryce-Jones, New York Herald Tribune

If you wish to receive details of forthcoming publications,
please send your address to
Eland Books, 53 Eland Road, London SW11 5JX

Previously published by
ELAND BOOKS

TRAVELS INTO THE INTERIOR OF AFRICA

MUNGO PARK

With a new preface by Jeremy Swift

Famous triumphs of exploration have rarely engendered outstanding books. *Travels into the Interior of Africa*, which has remained a classic since its first publication in 1799, is a remarkable exception.

It was a wonder that he survived so long, and a still greater one that his diaries could have been preserved . . . what amazing reading they make today!
Roy Kerridge, Tatler

The enthusiasm and understanding which informs Park's writing is irresistible.
Frances Dickenson, Time Out

One of the greatest and most respected explorers the world has known, a man of infinite courage and lofty principles, and one who dearly loved the black African.
E. W. Bovill, the Niger Explored

Told with a charm and naivety in themselves sufficient to captivate the most fastidious reader . . . modesty and truthfulness peep from every sentence . . . for actual hardships undergone, for dangers faced, and difficulties overcome, together with an exhibition of virtues which make a man great in the rude battle of life. Mungo Park stands without a rival.
Joseph Thomson, author of Through Masailand

*If you wish to receive details of forthcoming publications,
please send your address to
Eland Books, 53 Eland Road, London SW11 5JX*

A CURE FOR SERPENTS

THE DUKE OF PIRAJNO
An Italian doctor in North Africa

The Duke of Pirajno arrived in North Africa in 1924. For the next eighteen years, his experiences as a doctor in Libya, Eritrea, Ethiopia, and Somaliland provided him with opportunities and insights rarely given to a European. He brings us stories of noble chieftains and celebrated prostitutes, of Berber princes and Tuareg entertainers, of giant elephants and a lioness who fell in love with the author.

He tells us story after story with all the charm and resource of Scheherazade herself.
Harold Nicolson, Observer

A delightful personality, warm, observant, cynical and astringent. . .Doctors who are good raconteurs make wonderful reading.
Cyril Connolly, Sunday Times

A very good book indeed. . .He writes a rapid darting natural prose, like the jaunty scutter of a lizard on a rock.
Maurice Richardson, New Statesman

Pirajno's book is a cure for a great deal more than serpents.
The Guardian

In the class of book one wants to keep on a special shelf.
Doris Lessing, Good Book Guide

If you wish to receive details of forthcoming publications,
please send your address to
Eland Books, 53 Eland Road, London SW11 5JX

NUNAGA

DUNCAN PRYDE
Ten years among the Eskimos

Duncan Pryde, an eighteen-year-old orphan, an ex-merchant-seaman, and disgruntled factory worker left Glasgow for Canada to try his hand at fur-trading.

He became so absorbed in this new life that his next ten years were spent living with the Eskimos. He became part of their life even in its most intimate manifestations: hunting, shamanism, wife-exchange and blood feuds.

This record of these years is not only an astonishing adventure, but an unrivalled record of a way of life which, along with the igloo, has vanished altogether.

He tells us stories, which he seems to have been born to do.
Time

One of the best books about Arctic life ever written . . . A marvellous story, well told.
Sunday Times

If you wish to receive details of forthcoming publications,
please send your address to
Eland Books, 53 Eland Road, London SW11 5JX

Previously published by
ELAND BOOKS

THE LAW

A novel by
ROGER VAILLAND

With a new preface by Jonathan Keates

The Law is a cruel game that was played in the taverns of Southern Italy. It reflects the game of life in which the whole population of Manacore is engaged. Everyone from the feudal landowner, Don Cesare, to the landless day-labourers are participants in the never-ending contest.

Every paragraph and every section of this novel has been carefully cast and seems to be locked into position, creating a structure which is solid and formal, yet always lively. . .while we are reading the novel its world has an absolute validity. . . *The Law* is an experience I will not easily forget.
V. S. Naipaul, New Statesman

The Law deserves every reading it will have. It is and does all that a novel should – amuses, absorbs, excites and illuminates not only its chosen patch of ground but much more of life and character as well.
New York Times

One feels one knows everyone in the district. . .every page has the texture of living flesh.
New York Herald Tribune

A full rich book teeming with ambition, effort and desire as well as with ideas.
Times Literary Supplement

If you wish to receive details of forthcoming publications, please send your address to Eland Books, 53 Eland Road, London SW11 5JX